AF470973

THE GREASEPAINT WAR

Show Business 1939-45

THE GREASEPAINT WAR

Show Business 1939–45

John Graven Hughes

NEW ENGLISH LIBRARY
TIMES MIRROR

First published in Great Britain by New English Library, Barnard's Inn, Holborn, London EC1N 2JR in 1976.

Printed in Great Britain by Thomson Litho, East Kilbride.
Bound by Hunter & Foulis, Edinburgh.

4500 30644

CONTENTS

ACKNOWLEDGEMENTS

A great many people have helped in my research for this book – far too many to mention individually. And I thank them all. I must thank the Imperial War Museum, London for giving me access to material on ENSA; Emlyn Williams for giving me the run of his unique collection of wartime clippings; Ralph Reader and Bill Sutton for information on RAF *Gang Shows*; Theo Cowan and Sue Hyman for arranging interviews; Fred Emney for his advice and Fay Mehlman for her secretarial assistance.

I also acknowledge permission to include the quotation from *My Wicked, Wicked Ways* by Errol Flynn published by Heinemann.

The quotation on page 73 is included by permission of *The Morning Star* newspaper.

Finally, if there is to be a dedication for *The Greasepaint War* it must be to those people who worked in the wartime theatre but who are no longer by our side, and to my wife Ruby for her unfailing understanding and assistance.

JGH

FOREWORD

In the early part of 1942 I received a cunningly worded invitation to join the army, and having nothing better to do at the time I decided to accept.

I shall never forget that first day, standing – with brave confidence and butterflies in the stomach – in a long line with a lot of other chaps, and being suddenly confronted by a large man whom I took to be Boris Karloff in one of his more fiendish roles. He turned out to be the regimental-sergeant-major.

Marching straight up to me he said, 'What's your number?'

I told him, 'Mayfair 0576.'

He then addressed me in a language I had never heard before, but I soon picked it up. It was British army basic English which appeared to consist of one monotonously repetitive word.

The next thing I remember was going into the exquisitely appointed dining-hall for a meal, after which I innocently complimented the chef on his devilish ingenuity and superior knowledge of the culinary arts.

No! It wasn't a bit like that. In fact the army provided me with a marvellous opportunity to try out as a raconteur – but look, I'd better pass you over to John Graven Hughes who tells you exactly what it was really like.

I do hope you enjoy it. Cheers.

Terry-Thomas, 1976

PREFACE

I remember as a small boy, growing up in the London suburb of Eltham just before World War II, being taken to the Royal Artillery Theatre, Woolwich to see the pantomime, *Cinderella*. Sitting in the gallery, rather out of place in my first pair of long white trousers and green school blazer with 'St Joseph's Academy Blackheath' neatly embroidered in yellow on the breast-pocket, I was entranced with the entire production from the opening chorus to the last lines spoken by the principal girl across the blue and amber footlights.

> And so dear friends our story ends;
> Its moral you can guess.
> So from all of us to everyone,
> … Good luck and happiness.

Although I have no memory of the songs that were sung and no idea who was in the show, I do remember thinking what a great life it must be to work in the theatre all the time.

Early in September 1939 I was sent away to school in the south of Ireland and by the time I was ready for the university entrance exam my family had moved to Dublin where father was appointed architect to the Board of Works. He decided, as fathers tended to do in those days, that I should eventually follow in his formidable footsteps and he put me into the Architectural Faculty of the National University. As I foolishly neglected to attend most of the lectures I naturally failed the first-year exams and was forced to look around for some other career.

It was largely through the advice and encouragement of another student and part-time actor Dan O'Herlihy that I was able to join Longford Productions at the Gate Theatre to play walk-ons for £1 a week in plays like *Oedipus Rex*, *Hamlet* and *The Seagull*.

Towards the end of 1943, with World War II well into its stride, I joined ENSA in Northern Ireland together with a handful of Dublin actors that included Wilfrid Brambell and Edward Mulhare, and we spent the next two years touring the garrison towns of Ulster, putting on plays in places with names like Ballymoney, Ballykelly, Fivemiletown and Sixmilecross. We celebrated victory in Europe (and my nineteenth birthday) with the RAF at Castle Archdale and V-J Day with the Fleet Air Arm at Maydown, by the shores of Lough Foyle.

In November 1945, I toured the Middle East with an ENSA production of *Pink String and Sealing Wax*. On my return to London I managed to join the cast of one of the last shows to be sent out from Drury Lane, *The Wind and the Rain*, which we played to the 'Bevin Boys' working in the mining villages of Stafford and Nottinghamshire.

And so, like many other actors, I served a kind of theatrical apprenticeship, working in front of service audiences. It was much later – when I was at Pinewood Studios in the 1960s as an extra in the crowd scenes of the film *Cleopatra* – that I finally decided I should try some other, less precarious way of earning a living.

When given the opportunity to start the research for this book over two years ago I discovered that many of today's established stars who had begun in the theatre during World War II had almost complete recall of those years. It is their memories that form the bulk of *The Greasepaint War*.

John Graven Hughes, 1976

The solemn temples, the great globe itself,
Yea, all which it inherit, shall dissolve
And like this insubstantial pageant faded,
Leave not a rack behind.

The Tempest: Act IV, 1

It all began in a drifting downward summer-slide of days when Deanna Durbin made her *First Love*; when little Shirley Temple sailed aboard the Good Ship Lollipop and Clark Gable promised to love, honour and obey Carole Lombard before going back to the studio to inform Scarlett O'Hara that frankly he didn't give a damn.

A time when King Kong, Lassie and Pluto the pup were pipped at the post by such glittering stars as Jane Russell and Betty Grable.

George Bernard Shaw won an Oscar for *Pygmalion* which was produced by Gabriel Pascal, the man who made *Major Barbara* and *Caesar and Cleopatra*, and who died penniless in New York trying to raise the money to launch a new musical with the whimsical title of *My Fair Lady*.

A time, too, when prospects were bleak and fears were allayed with political platitudes. Trenches were dug and gas-masks issued, and the harsh voice of Hitler rose to a higher chord as he planted his pitchfork in the twentieth century and planned to crack open the Continent like a porcelain piggy bank.

In London during the summer of 1939 the most popular plays appeared to be those dealing with middle-class life, written with condescension in the comic idiom, concerned with wicked weekend escapades in English country houses, and containing the kind of back-chat now only encountered on television in *Coronation Street*.

The young at heart shouldered each other aside to watch *The Dancing Years* at Drury Lane; the rest queued for Alice Delysia at the Criterion in *French for Love*, or Stanley Lupino in *The Fleet's Lit Up* at the Hippodrome.

Binnie Hale and Bea Lillie and the debonair Jack Buchanan smiled and sang and sparkled like the Coca-Cola sign in Piccadilly Circus, and the hit show of the decade was called *Me and My Girl*.

You could find them all doing 'The Lambeth Walk' with dogged zeal and Lupino Lane twice nightly at the Victoria Palace, and the Noel Gay number outsold every other popular song of the period apart from 'Yes, We Have No Bananas'; it eventually became top of the pops in every palais from Portland Bill to Pentland Firth.

It was a very good year for the cinema with films like *The Story of Vernon and Irene Castle* with Ginger Rogers and the agile Fred Astaire; *Goodbye Mr Chips* with Robert Donat and Greer Garson and an impressive piece of propaganda from Warner Brothers, *Confessions of a Nazi Spy*, starring Edward G. Robinson and George Sanders.

Although Gracie Fields and George Formby – both from mill towns north of Manchester – were voted Britain's top box-office stars, housewives preferred to spend an hour or two at an afternoon matinée with the laconic Gary Cooper, knowing implicitly that the clear eye, the granite profile and the implacable cool were the result of a good clean life.

The popularity of news cinemas took an upward curve the year after Munich with newsreels showing – as a contrast to royalty looking better than ever – Europe sliding towards the brink of war while Chamberlain chatted to Mussolini in Rome, the British ambassador bowed from a balcony in

Warsaw, and French General Weygand flushed with pride as he inspected the line of supposedly impregnable fortifications on the eastern frontier named in honour of War Minister André Maginot.

But events moved with startling swiftness, and crisis followed crisis with monotonous regularity. Not many people believed in the summer of 1939 that the storm would blow itself out, and below the surface optimism was a feeling of inevitability and the fear that things would probably get worse.

On the first day of September newspaper headlines read: DON'T PANIC, DIG, and lovers having a final fling may have fallen into freshly dug shelter trenches in Hyde Park. Word got out that Hitler had finally attacked Poland, and before you could say Ivor Novello, dim drums throbbed to the ominous rhythm of martial music. Democracy went on the defensive. Hundreds of thousands of children were bundled out of London and other major cities and sent into the country or to so-called safe areas like Dover and Deal, coastal resorts which later attracted the attention of enemy bombs.

It was time for angels to find less dangerous places in which to dine, and the sound heard above the roar of the traffic in Berkeley Square was a nightingale clearing its throat through a gas-mask.

Earlier on that Friday in September, Nazi troops had stormed across the Polish frontier, Warsaw experienced its first air-raid, and in Britain every able-bodied man between eighteen and forty-one became liable for call-up.

The BBC packed up its cameras and closed down its pioneer television service. Anxious crowds waited in Downing Street. They realised that with the dropping of those German bombs on Poland, conditions had changed overnight. The old world was beginning to break up for good and all, and it meant that the lives of countless families were to be disrupted. Naturally the first to be uprooted from home and separated from parents were the children.

To six-year-old Maurice Joseph Micklewhite it seemed

the end of everything. This son of a Billingsgate fish porter and a Cockney charwoman was then living in Urlwin Street near the Elephant and Castle (less than half a mile from Pownell Terrace where Charlie Chaplin spent his childhood), in the industrial wasteland across the Thames from Westminster. He never forgot the morning he took up his cardboard-boxed gas-mask and said goodbye to his mother before setting off to join the rest of the children in the playground of Peckham Grammar School.

Internationally known today as Michael Caine, film actor of distinctive charm, he remembers all those years ago standing with his little mate Clarence, the terror of the roller-skate set, at the tail-end of the school crocodile as they began the long walk to the railway station.

'We passed all these women standing at their front gates shaking their heads and telling us not to worry; we'd be back home by Christmas. Personally I didn't think I'd ever see the Elephant again.'

As the grey and navy-blue tide poured into the main road to stern cries of 'Steady, boys, steady!' from the imperious masters, Clarence sidestepped to avoid a passing tram and very nearly fell under the hooves of a brewery dray horse. Caine continued: 'The train dropped us off miles from anywhere and we were lined up in a village hall like tiny Toby Jugs at an antique auction while all the local women walked past weighing us up. Clarence and me were left behind at the end.

'As the authorities muttered among themselves and debated the possibility of putting the two of us back on the next train to London, a spiky old girl with a distinct resemblance to a bat came up and asked how much money she'd get for taking us. The only thing I remember about staying at her house was the RSPCC coming along after two days to collect us; she wasn't giving us enough to eat.'

Kenneth Williams also lined up for inspection in a school hall in a strange town where local people picked out the children they wanted. Like Michael Caine he was still there at the end, and recalls being handed over to the district nurse for the night.

Williams recalls: 'When I asked her with characteristic modesty why no one had chosen me she snapped, "Because you've got such a nasty little sneer on your face, that's why!" Even the army couldn't obliterate it; it was still evident whenever there was a kit inspection. But it came in useful after the war when I decided to become a professional actor.'

Les Dawson, living at home in a seedy part of Manchester, was evacuated to the world-famous resort of Blackpool with a large party of very small children.

'There was another boy in the same billet with spots all over his face and only one shirt to his name. It was so filthy the foster-parents found it impossible to wash so he was taken out to the backyard every Saturday night and decontaminated. I was only there a few months and can't remember a great deal apart from the food. From the way it was cooked I'd say the family were directly descended from the Borgias.'

With war inevitable, thousands of children were sent across the Atlantic to safety, among them a pretty little girl of seven who left her comfortable home above Hampstead Heath to settle with her mother—former actress Sara Sothern—on the more commanding heights of Beverly Hills.

Her father, a prosperous art dealer on first-name terms with most of the film tycoons, would have taken his daughter sightseeing through glens and canyons full of lush tropical vegetation to show her the stunning collection of handsome homes with paved patios, picture windows and private pools, and set among giant pepper and eucalyptus trees.

She would have marvelled at the ornamental hotels, restaurants and upper-bracket department stores located between Wilshire and Santa Monica Boulevards, and perhaps paused on the forecourt of that familiar landmark and tourist attraction, Grauman's Chinese Theatre, to match her small handprints with those of stars like Barbara Stanwyck, Loretta Young, Tyrone Power and Humphrey Bogart. She may have waited to cross the street at the corner of Hollywood and Vine – where Garbo once walked in trousers to begin a new era in world fashion for women – and she might have eaten her first American hamburger in the very same Schwab's Drugstore where Lana Turner was discovered.

Exposed early to fresh orange juice, hot buttered popcorn in front of big log fires, and clambakes on sandy beaches, the little girl also went to school with the offsprings of the couplings of beautiful women and tanned athletic men, all of them secure in the knowledge that the world was full of people whose eyes had no other function but to light up at the sight of them. These celebrated performers were unaware that the golden age of Hollywood was drawing to a close and fortunately World War II (although it brought problems: the materials for film production were drastically cut) heralded an unprecedented boom period for the cinema.

It also ushered in a brand-new teenage group known as 'bobbysoxers', who were to clamour for fresher and much younger stars – such as Elizabeth Taylor. That curiously resilient actress made her first movie for Universal when she was nine, and appeared in MGM's *Lassie Come Home*, two years later. Later she saw Hollywood as the place that stole her childhood away: 'and I've had to try and catch up on my education ever since'.

In contrast, Richard (Burton) Jenkins was fourteen in September 1939 and attending school at Port Talbot, a Welsh conurbation of iron, steel, copper and coal spread along the eastern fringe of Swansea Bay. His life had become something other than secure at a very early age; his mother died when he was two and he was sent to live with his sister and her miner husband at Taibach, a collection of terraced backstreets above Port Talbot, and not far from his birthplace of Pontrhydyfen where his father and other members of the family lived frugally.

The first time that great voice with the rich timbre of a finely tuned cello was heard to any effect was in his school's production of Shaw's *The Apple Cart*, and it proved to be Burton's springboard into the theatre. The producer was English teacher and spare-time radio scriptwriter Phillip Burton, who later adopted him, and with hours of tuition in voice production and control encouraged him to think in terms of the theatre as a career. It was the English teacher who noticed Emlyn Williams's advertisement for Welsh actors for his new play *The Druid's Rest* in 1943, and as a result of a successful audition, Richard Burton became a professional actor at eighteen years of age.

Another young Welsh boy from Ferndale in the Rhondda Valley also attended the audition 'simply to get out of the valleys'. He was in the play when it opened in Liverpool on 22 November 1943. The self-assured and highly competitive Stanley Baker badly needed the security of achievement. The son of a miner who had lost a leg in a colliery accident and with brothers still at school, he belonged to what was known as a 'Means Test' family. This meant an inquiry into their income to determine eligibility for benefit – a political hot potato since 1933 when the Ramsay MacDonald government proposed that unemployment benefit at the height of the depression should be graded according to need.

Baker recalled: 'I was dressed in the uniform of the poor, head shaved like a convict with a fringe at the front, rough grey wool jersey and short trousers with bloody great patches . . . and the boots, bloody great clodhoppers always a size too large. It was never for me a question of being top man in the sense of bossing around those lower down. I wanted the independence of wealth so that when the crunch came I could always preserve my own integrity.'

For some evacuees the war was the turning-point in their lives, for others it was simply a time of unhappiness and insecurity. For all of them it meant growing up in a world just beginning to creak back and forth on its hinges like an unlatched gate in a force-nine wind.

For Emlyn Williams the approaching war meant the closure of his play *The Corn Is Green*. The same evening that children were being sent out of London, he stepped in front of the safety curtain to ask the handful of people in the audience if they'd like to move nearer the footlights where his company could help them forget the crisis for a couple of hours. It was the same on the next night, Saturday, and then came Sunday, 3 September. Chamberlain spoke to the nation over the radio, telling them that he had asked Germany to undertake to withdraw her troops from Poland but 'I have to tell you that no such undertaking has been received and that consequently this country is at war with Germany'.

With the false alarm of an air-raid siren, time snapped suddenly – a steel cable strained beyond the limits of its endurance, and the country prepared to face the holocaust.

As London braced itself for the expected savage assault from the air, one by one the shutters slammed on the theatres and plans for new productions, indefinitely postponed, were posted on the billboards of history. Although the official shut-down only lasted a week, with the shadow of Goering's *Luftwaffe* over the West End it was the end of long-running successes like *Dear Octopus* and *Goodness, How Sad,* and the shock of sudden unemployment for established stars like Edith Evans, Margaret Rutherford, John Gielgud and Robert Morley.

It made that perverse old soul George Bernard Shaw profoundly indignant, particularly when the German air-force failed to show up and the Sitzkrieg (or 'phoney war') began. With one fiery eye on vanished royalties he wanted to know 'what agent of Hitler was it who suggested we all cower in the darkness for the duration?'

He suggested that the authorities should immediately set to work and provide new theatres where they were lacking and 'all actors, variety artistes, musicians and entertainers should be exempted from every form of active service except their own all-important one'.

Authority, benighted by orders, disorders and counter-commands, ignored his suggestions and busied itself with blackouts, barrage balloons and the sandbagging of statues dedicated to the dashing heroes of World War I. Un-employed entertainers, on the other hand, felt that the playwright had made a valid point.

It was Ernest Hemingway who said, with his gift for cogent simplicity, that if you wanted to know something about World War II you should get someone who was there to tell you about it.

Like Barbara Stewart. In 1939 she was a fifteen-year-old chorus-girl in Jack Hylton's *Band Waggon* at the London Palladium, sharing a dressing-room in the lulls between kicking the 'Can-Can' and dancing the 'Boomps-a-Daisy' – 'with dignity, discretion and decorum'.

The girls were looking forward to a reasonably long run, but one sunny afternoon in August, as they were all giggling and grumbling and changing costumes, a couple of workmen walked into the room with ladders, brushes and a tin of black paint.

'During that week', Barbara said, 'we naturally wondered what would happen if there was a war. We were terrified when they blacked-out all the windows because it meant they were expecting air-raids. Then on Saturday, 2 September, after the second house, we were told the show was closing. We were all out of work and there was nothing for us until pantomime rehearsals started in December.'

Band Waggon, adapted from a radio series, starred Arthur Askey, Richard Murdoch and Tommy Trinder. A highlight of the show was Bryan Michie's 'Youth Takes a Bow', com-pèred by Trinder, which introduced some exciting juvenile talent including a buoyant little thirteen year old who bounced on and sang, accompanied by Billy Ternent's orchestra, 'Let's Have a Tiddly at the Milk Bar'. He was billed as Ernest Wise, singer and dancer.

The only thing Tommy Trinder can remember today about *Band Waggon* was the 'Boomps-a-Daisy': 'and after all my years in the business I finally made the Palladium to see my name in lights and what happened? Along came the blackout.'

On 3 September he was booked for a Sunday concert at Bridlington and listened to the car radio as he drove out of London: 'I knew if it was war there'd be no show and as soon as I heard the news I stopped to turn back and very nearly collided with a coach-load of expectant mothers. "Blimey," I told the driver, "what a time you've had; no wonder you left London." Then the siren went and they all waddled out to stand in a flooded shelter, up to their maternity belts in water.

'An air-raid warden ordered me to join them in what I felt was a rather peremptory tone of voice. "With that lot?" I asked, "Not on your flippin' life mate. I'd rather be bombed." I got back in the car and drove home.'

Impersonator Florence Desmond, expecting a baby in the autumn, had been booked to appear in *Band Waggon* but a severe haemorrhage forced her to leave the show during rehearsals. She spent the first morning of the war packing valuable china away in her new house at Hampstead while her husband Charles Hughesdon went to church as usual.

'As soon as I heard that siren I ran down to tell the German cook to take shelter and found her flinging herself about the kitchen in such a frenzy I feared for the Crown Derby.

'"*Oh mein lieber Gott*," she was wailing, "my brudder is in der *Luftwaffe* and he could be on top of us zis minute waiting to drop his bombs . . ."

'Charles came back in time to see me land a right hook on the point of her chin. I was more scared than she was but it worked. She shut up.'

Terry-Thomas, at this time, was enjoying a modest success in cabaret 'until that blackguard Hitler interrupted me. I was working the fleshpots of Northampton that week and was

driving back with Hutch—radio's "Prince of Melody"—
when we heard the air-raid warning as we approached
Finchley. I'd been born in the beastly place but I had no
intention of dying there, so I suggested we should make a
surreptitious beeline for the North Circular Road and keep
going until we got back to town.

'As things turned out, the war gave me a wonderful chance
to work on my comedy act and it wasn't long before I was
doing three shows a day for the forces ... until I became a
soldier myself.'

Bebe Daniels and Ben Lyon were in Blackpool and,
according to Ben, they 'didn't know what the hell to do'.
Eventually they decided to return to London. 'As soon as we
spotted those barrage balloons,' recalls Ben Lyon, 'we both
got the shakes; we were sure the sky would be black with
German bombers any minute but it was weird. No sign of
aircraft and Londoners going about their business as though
nothing unusual had happened.'

Beryl Reid began in variety shortly before September
1939, playing dates like Bridlington and Blackpool for £2
a week. She was at Saltburn-by-the-Sea when war was
declared, doing a summer season on the end of the pier:
'It was heartbreaking really. The glamour of it all just
beginning for me and I had to pack my make-up, pay my
digs and walk to the station to catch a train back home to
Manchester. Fortunately I wasn't out of work too long and
my first date when the theatres opened again was at the
Floral Hall, Scarborough with the Western Brothers.'

With air-raids imminent Mrs Kerr-Trimmer wanted her
daughter back home in Mayfield, Sussex, but she insisted
on staying to finish the season at Regent's Park Open-Air
Theatre.

'I had been training to be a ballet dancer,' said Deborah
Kerr, 'but my father, crippled in World War I, became ill
again so I was sent to a boarding school near Bristol where
my Aunt Jane taught drama.

'She was a great influence and taught me so much about

the theatre. When I was studying at Sadler's Wells in 1939 I auditioned for Robert Atkins and he engaged me for Regent's Park.'

Agent John Gliddon (who discovered Vivien Leigh) saw Miss Kerr play a lady-in-waiting in *As You Like It*. He suggested there might be a big future for her in pictures, a notion that fell a trifle lamely on the ear of Miss Kerr: 'As far as I was concerned in those days pictures meant remote Hollywood stars like Garbo and Gable and quite honestly the thought of being in films myself never crossed my mind. At least not until I met John Gliddon again. After the Open-Air Theatre closed I was staying at the YWCA hostel near Tottenham Court Road and quite by chance bumped into Robert Atkins. He said, "Where on earth have you been hiding, my child? Gliddon's been looking for you everywhere."

'And that's how it started. I was introduced to Michael Powell and he gave me a walk-on in *Contraband*, then in production at Denham Studios. I learnt valuable lessons in screen make-up and camera technique and the experience led to a test in another picture. Because the war had just begun I got a great deal of publicity as the first blackout film star.'

Michael Powell, who worked with Emeric Pressburger, became one of Britain's best-known directors. In *Contraband*, a well-made espionage movie, he made good use of London locations against a background of air-raid precautions, blackout and civil defence.

Not long after *Contraband* was finished, Deborah Kerr was lunching with a friend at the Savoy, and by a happy coincidence the flamboyant film director Gabriel Pascal was at an adjoining table.

He was explaining to an associate his difficulty trying to find an actress to play the innocent 'Jenny Hill' in his next production, Shaw's *Major Barbara*, when he suddenly stopped and looked across the restaurant, wild surmise lighting up his eyes.

'Look at that face,' he said, and in the finest Hollywood tradition he rose from the table and went over to place a paternal hand on the shoulder of a somewhat startled Deborah Kerr. 'Tell me, sweet virgin,' he said in an accent of indeterminate origin, 'are you an actress? I need an innocent young girl for my next picture.'

Blushing, she lifted her head and, giving him a very searching look indeed, she admitted that she was an actress. He arranged for a test and she was cast as Jenny Hill in *Major Barbara*, working with a number of leading players including Wendy Hiller—following up her success in *Pygmalion*—Sybil Thorndike, Emlyn Williams and Rex Harrison.

One night at the end of World War I a versatile, if eccentric, comedian called Laurie Howe finished his act and left the stage of the Palladium to find a message from the other half of the act, his wife Bertha Callen, awaiting him. It simply said, 'I feel a son coming on.' The comedian jumped into a cab and hurried along to the University College Hospital in time to greet his new-born son with the words, 'My God! Isn't it ugly?'

Richard Gilbert Emery was to know unhappiness, poverty and deprivation. When he was eight years old his parents split up, and he lived in a one-room flat in Hampstead with his mother on an income that averaged £1 a week.

'As soon as I was old enough,' says Dick Emery, 'I wanted to go into the theatre but my mother advised me against it. I did all kinds of jobs including a spell as a driving instructor and at the same time I developed what I hoped could become a fine tenor voice.

'For a long time it had been my ambition to go to Italy and study under Tetrazzini (the world-famous singing teacher who died in 1940) but the war came along and messed everything up.

'I'd done a little work in the provincial theatre and even

won a talent contest at the Grange cinema in Kilburn, but it was nothing to set the world on fire. I was too nervous and it affected everything I tried to do. Anyway I was called up in the RAF. Fully intending to be a pilot, I ended up peeling spuds down at Halton as an aircrafthand, general duties. I hated any form of discipline in those days and it took an awful long time to settle down.

'It's strange when you think it was probably the finest thing that could have happened; I was able to audition for Ralph Reader's *Gang Show* and the experience was absolutely invaluable. All those television characters were inside me, even then, merely waiting to be developed.'

And at the beginning of World War II, Gracie Fields was in her new villa on the Isle of Capri, enjoying her first real vacation: 'With no scripts in sight and no concert bookings to worry about it was going to be wonderful. Then along came that Sunday and all the lights went off in Naples Harbour.

'I knew it was time to lock up the Canzone del Mare and head for home. As far as I knew, they'd need me to entertain the forces the way I did in World War I. I daresay it would be the same today. I'd still go round the hospitals if they wanted me. You see, they've always been a part of my life, soldiers from wars.'

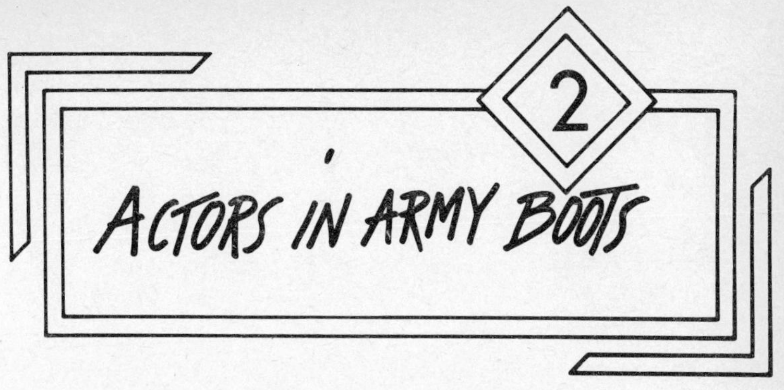

Beds will be made up as laid down in standing orders
Notice in RAF Airmen's Quarters

As the Welsh dawn threw pale-blue shadows over the frosted slopes of the Mumbles Peninsula a train, full of civilians in scratchy khaki uniforms on their way to war, pulled slowly out of Swansea station. There was no glittering pomp, no brass band–only the whistle of the engine echoing in the morning air. Inside the end compartment harassed-looking men tried to read newspapers in the dim light, and a dimpled little territorial from St Thomas's Estate, full of hope and belief in the future, turned to the red-eyed recruit sitting miserably in the corner.

'On our way at last, boy,' he said, beaming through his glasses. 'This is more like it, eh?'

His companion gave him a bleak look and went on staring out at the drab streets.

Gunner Secombe tried another approach. 'Any idea where we're going?'

The soldier shrugged and slumped down in the dusty seat.

A few minutes later Gunner Secombe nudged him in the ribs. 'Join the army and see the world, eh? You know, we could end up anywhere. Perhaps even the Middle East. Imagine lying on smooth sand bleached white by the hot sun, listening to the sound of the Mediterranean with the air spiced like wine, full of the elusive scent of lemon trees ...'

'You can shove it,' said the recruit abruptly. 'Sod seeing the world.'

The train rumbled into Neath station and as it stopped alongside the platform, sergeants and corporals with a remarkable talent for invective began running up and down pulling carriage doors open and screaming at the disconsolate soldiers who gathered they were to pick up their effing luggage and get effing well fell in outside on the effing road.

'The Middle East,' sneered the boy in the corner with ill-disguised relish. 'Looks to me more like bloody Merthyr Tydfil.'

Harry Secombe, his first fine ecstasy of patriotism evaporating like ice-cream left out in the Gobi Desert at noon, began his basic training building latrines on a half-acre of fertile Welsh soil seven miles from home.

'Then about four in the morning,' he remembers, 'a herd of NCOs thundered through the billet shouting ear-splitting obscenities at us as we lay sleeping in our service-issue palliasses. I shook like a jelly at bay and in two seconds I was standing at the foot of the bed in singlet and shorts crying "God for Harry, England and Saint George."

'Fortunately the other chaps gradually grew to appreciate my daunting eccentricities. It's strange how there's always at least one funny man in every bunch to leaven the mix and cheer things up whenever total apathy threatens. I learned to create comedy out of macabre situations in the army, and I had the chance to try myself out in front of a ready-made audience. They were my raw material and the family twit from the St Thomas's Estate became the battery idiot. The more I fooled about the more confidence I gained, especially when I took my glasses off. I used to fall over things and that always got a laugh.

'We weren't at Neath more than a fortnight when we were sent back home; there was nowhere to post us. This kind of thing happened so often I didn't dare set foot in the town. By then a lot of the boys who had waved me off were fighting in France, so I spent days skulking along the back streets of Swansea, but there was always some eagle-eyed mother who spotted me: "Hello Harry, how is it you're not over there then with all the rest of the lads?"

'In desperation I went into the Royal Artillery depot and begged them to send me anywhere as long as it was away from home.

'I was issued with tropical kit, inoculated against prickly heat, beri-beri and jungle fever and posted to Usk, twenty-three miles from Cardiff. If it wasn't exactly at the cannon's mouth at least it was under canvas.'

Towards the end of September, feet in heavy army boots were tramping all over England's mountains green as all the young conscripts prepared to walk a million miles for one of their sergeants' smiles. The National Service Act of 1939 (which was later extended to include men of fifty-one and unmarried women between twenty and thirty) which ordered them into uniform came as either a calamity of biblical proportions or an answer to prayer; thousands of people were drawn into the war before they had properly embarked on a career.

Exemption from military service could be claimed on grounds of religious or other beliefs, and 60,000 claimed it. About 3,500 were given unconditional exemption; 15,000 were allowed to perform non-combatant duties with the army, and 29,000 were exempted so long as they worked in agriculture.

Some of today's top entertainers were only starting to climb the minor foothills of show business in 1939, others were merely talented amateurs, and a substantial number were given unparalleled opportunities to develop as individual performers able to exploit whatever talent they possessed in front of thousands of troops in the different theatres of war.

Laurence (now Lord) Olivier was one of the many established actors who went into the services. He came back from

Hollywood to become a lieutenant in the Fleet Air Arm.

Posted to Worthy Down in May 1941, he became parachute officer partly through the good offices of his friend Lieutenant-Commander Ralph Richardson, then supervising parachute maintenance on all shore-based stations. He paid a visit to Worthy Down to see how Olivier was getting on and found no fault at all; his section was efficient, everything was in good order, and he seemed to know each of his men by name as well as rank.

One thought did cross Richardson's mind as he left the station: 'I wonder if he rehearsed it all?'

David Niven also came back from Hollywood to join the RAF, but finding no welcome there he enlisted in the Rifle Brigade and later became a colonel on General Eisenhower's staff.

Sir Michael Redgrave served briefly as an ordinary seaman before he was invalided out of the Royal Navy and another sailor, David Jacobs, became a senior announcer on the forces Radio SEAC (South-east Asia Command), taking over from McDonald Hobley.

Kenneth More spent six years altogether in the navy: 'It was a very busy time in places all over the world. I lost some good friends and also made a lot of new friends. I kept well clear of entertainment during my service apart from running the ship's concert party; I felt I should keep my profession entirely separate. I was a naval officer on active duty and the theatre had no part in it.

'When the war was over I believe I was a better actor for having been on active service than if I had missed it. For one thing, it taught me a great deal about humanity.'

Leo Genn, who had qualified as a barrister before becoming an actor in the West End, was a lieutenant-colonel in charge of an officer-training depot; in 1945 he was one of the prosecuting counsel during the Nuremberg War Crimes trials. Richard Todd was commissioned in the Parachute Regiment and Derek Bond was in the Grenadier Guards and saw action as an officer in Tunisia, where he won the Military Cross.

Coming from an Indian army family, Patrick Cargill was familiar with service life, but with both parents founder members of the Bexhill Theatre Society he hoped to make acting a full-time career.

'Unfortunately my elder brother was drowned while in the army in India and father asked if I'd give Sandhurst a try. I was commissioned and posted to India to join the 3/14th Punjabi Regiment and out there I helped with whatever shows were provided, but I wasn't happy with the life. After an illness in 1938 I decided to buy myself out and as soon as I got back to Bexhill I joined the repertory company at the De La Ware Pavilion.

'*Lot's Wife* was the first play and I had to tell the producer all my clothes were still on the way back from India. "That's OK," he said, "you're playing Adam. You won't need any clothes." Then war broke out. I was sure Hitler heard I'd left the army and decided to take a chance.'

Then he found himself in the awkward situation of being on the regular army reserve list with a War Office that stolidly refused to recall him to the colours.

'The theatre was taken over for the London evacuees then arriving in droves all along the south coast.

'They put me in charge of the lavatories and I spent the next few months knee-deep in urine. When several large-bosomed ladies in floral hats began flourishing white feathers at me in the street I realised I had to do something drastic, and I rejoined the army as a private in a signals unit at Wakefield. Destiny stepped in again when I was chosen for officer training at Catterick.

'I must be one of the few people left who has been through the ranks and promoted to lieutenant twice.'

During the West End run of the play *Tony Draws a Horse* in 1939, four members of the cast, Frank Lawton, Guy Middleton, Hugh Williams and Nigel Patrick joined the territorials.

'When the war started I was at the Comedy Theatre with

Lilian Braithwaite and Cyril Raymond,' said Nigel Patrick. 'I went off to the 2nd Battalion, Queen's Westminsters and immediately found myself guarding Staines Bridge for king, country and empire. Once commissioned I was gazetted to the 60th Rifles and after moving around a bit I went to headquarters, 30th Armoured Brigade in Yorkshire as senior liaison and entertainments officer. As there were more than 8,000 soldiers there and no cinema nearer than Malton, seventeen miles away, we put some pressure on the top brass and they got the divisional engineers to erect a theatre; Ian Carmichael was with me in the first production, *Springtime for Henry*.' (A student at the Royal Academy of Dramatic Art at the beginning of the war, Ian Carmichael ended it as a major in charge of troop entertainment in Germany.)

Colonel Patrick was eventually responsible for supplying shows to allied forces in southern Europe and North Africa: 'The war was a great experience. It's always been a tendency with young actors to believe the theatre is the only job worth bothering about, but I found it most rewarding to control such a vast amount of entertainment, for so many people. I gradually realised that other men's occupations were equally absorbing and I learned about administration; that was useful to me later in the profession.'

Broadcaster Jack de Manio was with the 7th Royal Sussex Regiment in the BEF (British Expeditionary Force) in France before Dunkirk. 'I had always wanted to be a soldier—the dressing-up and the colourful uniforms particularly appealed to me and the war was a crucial point in my life. I had little ambition, no idea what I was going to do and not much inclination to do anything.

'Because of the war I found myself in broadcasting and if there hadn't been a war I might have ended up as a bad head-waiter or a very good brewer. Perhaps I might have become a hotelier, I've always liked catering. Who knows, I might make one yet.'

He remembers a soldier who travelled to the Middle East with him being asked which place impressed him most and he replied: 'Cairo because the Naafi there was the best I've ever been in.'

That veteran of television's *Dad's Army*, Clive Dunn, did all he could to enlist but at the Central Recruiting Depot in London he was told to try the one at Edgware. Not having enough for the fare he next decided to give the navy a go; certainly they'd accept him, but only if he signed on for eight years. He thought about the RAF until someone told him he'd need a matriculation certificate and finally, showing exemplary enterprise, he joined the ambulance service to drive a commandeered Harrod's van around the city. When he did become a soldier later he was captured in Greece and sent to Austria where he organised prisoner-of-war concerts with necessarily all-male casts, including an Ivor Novello musical in which he played the female lead.

John Le Mesurier, who surprised his commanding officer by arriving ready for war in a cab with a set of golf-clubs among his personal baggage, was posted to the Far East and remembers being in Rangoon towards the end of the war 'where nothing got through at all, except Vera Lynn'.

If it hadn't been for World War II Arthur Lowe might never have had the chance to become an actor, although he 'might have joined an amateur group afterwards'.

'It's strange how life can turn out,' he says. 'I was a progress chaser with Fairey Aviation and could quite easily have claimed exemption, but as long ago as 1938 I was certain war was inevitable. I joined the Duke of Lancaster's Own Yeomanry in Manchester, chiefly because I was keen on horses. Then they took the animals away from us in 1940 and made us part of the Royal Artillery.'

But it wasn't until he was posted to a remote ordnance depot on the Gaza Strip that his involvement with services entertainment began.

Norman Wisdom, who made his professional stage debut at Collins Music Hall, London, in December 1946 as a £5-a-week stooge, was in India in 1935 as a band boy with the 10th Hussars and stayed in the army for the next ten years. A solo xylophonist with the regimental band (doubling trumpet and clarinet), he was anxious to extend his range as a performer, and in one concert he attempted a tap-dance in army boots and full uniform. The audience laughed at him so much he decided to become a comedian.

Another successful comedian had his first professional try-out at Collins after beginning in comedy by making army audiences laugh while serving in the Middle East. The son of a poultry farmer from Caerphilly, South Wales, Tommy Cooper was an apprentice shipwright at Southampton until he joined the Horse Guards in 1940, serving for seven years. He exercised horses in Hyde Park and did sentry duty in Whitehall before being posted to Egypt. He wore the traditional headgear, a tarboosh, while doing his act in concert party and it's been his trademark ever since. His wife Gwen is a former comedienne who toured during the war in ENSA shows with Tommy Trinder, but Cooper 'made her give it up. She was getting too good.'

After the war she worked in shops and offices, all kinds of jobs during the bad times when her husband was finding the going rough: 'But this is what separates the amateurs from the professionals, persistence. There are bound to be bad times and that's when so many people give up. I was determined to stick at it because I liked what I was doing and I have this streak of optimism. I work because it's enjoyable.'

Frankie Howerd, who had been sacked from his job as a clerk on London Docks and failed to get a scholarship to the Royal Academy of Dramatic Art as a result of a bad stammer and a formidable inferiority complex, was agreeably surprised when the Royal Artillery accepted him without question during the war.

In the army, he auditioned for ENSA and was rejected; four times he tried to get into the army's *Stars in Battledress* concert party, but each time his nervousness overcame him and he failed to make an impact: 'They didn't seem to think I was good enough even for Naafi concerts in those days.'

Then what made him believe he could stand up in front of crowds of people and entertain them? 'I wanted fame,' he said. 'I grew up thinking it would be the answer to all my problems. I realised I was an over-sensitive type who found it difficult to fit in anywhere. But it's the same with everything you think you want. When you finally get it, it never lives up to expectations.'

As a sergeant he landed in Normandy shortly after the invasion and saw service in France, Holland and Germany, still shy but learning what made audiences laugh. When he was demobbed he worked again briefly as a clerk and managed to get odd dates entertaining servicemen at the Nuffield Centre and the Stage Door Canteen. Signed up by an agent, it was the popular BBC series *Variety Bandbox* that established him as a comedian, and by 1950 he was starring at the London Palladium.

One man whose personality always conjures up a vision of the good old RAF in wartime with its beer-drinking, back-slapping bonhomie is Jimmy Edwards. He originally planned to be a teacher and taught at a preparatory school before studying at Cambridge for his MA degree. His father, a man in his sixties when Jimmy was a boy, was mathematics professor at the London University.

'I went straight into the RAF from Cambridge and because of my natural reticence I didn't get on too well with the other chaps at first. Then we were posted to Canada, and I gradually developed a keener taste for the whimsical. I still had difficulty adjusting to the hurly-burly of service life and rented a room in town with another chap who thought like me. We'd go there for a quiet read and to get away for a while from the ghastly barrack blocks.

'The whole boisterous thing really developed later, and that's when I got a taste for the entertainment business. As a well-known comedian one problem is that there seems to be no time off, as it were, for good behaviour. Complete strangers are firmly convinced they know you intimately and they always expect you to behave in a certain silly way, you know, loud, convivial and exhibitionistic, and there are so many times when that's the last thing you feel like being.'

When apprentice carpenter Wally Bygraves joined the RAF, as a fitter attached to Fighter Command, it was the first time he'd slept alone in a bed – apart from the twelve months spent convalescing from a childhood illness.

His family had moved to Rotherhithe from Bermondsey shortly before the war so that dad, an ex-professional boxer, could be nearer his work as a docker. Wally shared a bed with his father and brother, and his four sisters slept in the only other room with mum.

'How they ever managed to have children in those two rooms I'll never know. Not only that, we even put friends up from time to time.'

As a boy, young Bygraves sang a lot, already winning talent contests before he was twelve. He left school at fourteen to begin his apprenticeship.

He met his wife Blossom, then a WAAF sergeant, in the air-force and they married when he was nineteen, setting up their first home in a furnished room in Woolwich. 'One thing: I was determined never to go back to Rotherhithe again, at least not to live. I was aiming at a completely different, and I hoped, a much better sort of life when I came out of the RAF.'

Experience gained singing in RAF concerts gave him enough confidence to decide on show business as a career, and he'd also done some broadcasts on the BBC Forces programme. The reason he changed his name to 'Max' was because his Max Miller imitation had always gone down well during the war.

Harry Secombe remembers seeing Bygraves in the canteen at the BBC's Aeolian Hall in New Bond Street shortly after he was demobbed. 'We were all trying to break into the business and we used the canteen because the food was so much cheaper.

'I was sitting in there one lunchtime with Bill Kerr and Alfred Marks when this ex-RAF chap joined us and said what a hard time he was having, trying to get bookings. As he left the table he said: "Anyway I've kept my set of tools—I can always go back to carpentry for a living."'

It is probably safe to assume he finally disposed of his hammer and brace-and-bit as soon as he returned to London after touring in a revue called *For the Fun of It* with Frankie Howerd. Within weeks he was in the £120-a-week bracket and starring at the London Palladium.

Today the superbly assured incomparable Max Bygraves, who can make the lift of an eyebrow convey more than a ten-minute comedy routine, has a magnificent home at Bournemouth complete with a large pool, and a comfortable apartment on the ninth floor of a block of luxury high-rise flats in Victoria, overlooking the Thames . . . and the reaches of Rotherhithe.

For a few years before the war Bill Fraser ran a repertory company at Worthing, producing, directing and acting 'but it closed down in 1939 and I never got it back. When I joined the RAF I was able to get away from the theatre for a while to find how other people thought and talked, and I also found out about the kind of things that made them laugh.'

While waiting to be demobbed he formed a touring company to keep the troops entertained, and he discovered when he got back to his home station that he should have been out of the RAF two weeks before. Asked by his commanding officer what he planned to do in civilian life he muttered something about going back to the theatre.

'I don't fancy your chances, old boy,' said the CO. 'They've blown up all the piers, haven't they?'

He went straight into variety as a 'comic's labourer', working with traditional stars like Arthur Askey as well as up-and-coming personalities out of uniform like Tommy Cooper and Charlie Drake. Then came television, a comedy series called *The Army Game*, and his career as one of Britain's leading character-actors was established.

Charlie Drake himself was born near the Elephant and

Castle, and as a child he sold cats' meat door-to-door, as well as shovelling coal and doing a newspaper round; when he was eleven he started performing in the local clubs for an extra few shillings. In 1939 he was working at the headquarters of Naafi in Kennington, south London, and kept his job as a rock-cake mixer and oven man until he went into the RAF.

After the war, he played in clubs and small-time theatres, and then did a double-act with Jack Edwardes. They had a modest success both on television and in the theatre until 1957 when Charlie decided to become a single act, and then achieved television stardom in series like *The Worker* and *The Charlie Drake Show*.

Oldham-born Eric Sykes, 'a puny kid, always ill', sprang from poor but honest stock in the depressed twenties, and was at work at fourteen in a joiner's shop. Then followed a series of stop-gap occupations as a painter, greengrocer's assistant, office boy and a storekeeper in a cotton mill until the wartime RAF beckoned. He was taught a trade, qualifying as a wireless operator and got his first taste of show business in a station revue (produced by Flight-Lieutenant Bill Fraser). When the war ended the choice of career open to him appeared to be either to carry on doing revues for the troops or to go into the cookhouse. He chose entertainment, and in his spare time he wrote scripts on odd bits of paper with any old pencil-stub lying around.

A civilian again he worked briefly at the repertory theatre in Oldham and went on to gain further theatrical know-how in places like the Astoria, Llanelly with Frank H. Fortescue's Famous Players. Finally, hard-up and hungry, he managed to sell some comedy material to Frankie Howerd for *Variety Bandbox*, and he became a professional scriptwriter.

He was paid £15 an episode for the post-war radio success, *Educating Archie*, starring ventriloquist Peter Brough and his dummy Archie Andrews, and when he asked for a raise they told him he was 'pricing himself out of the business'. Nevertheless he was the first scriptwriter to earn £100 a week, and was at one time Europe's highest-paid comedy writer. His story since then, like others of that wartime breed of entertainers, is a glittering one of continuing success.

In the same air force, if more uneasily so, was the vigorous film director Ken Russell.

'The only good thing that happened to me was when I made friends with a very fat naval rating who'd been a ballet dancer and weighed over eighteen stone. We used to dance *pas de deux* together to gramophone records in the Naafi. So that's what I did in the war. I danced with a fat sailor.'

The Navy, Army and Air Force Institutes, or Naafi, which provides canteens for the forces, at home and abroad, is the successor to the Expeditionary Forces Canteens of World War I and even in peacetime it was a very big business. In vast warehouses at Kennington between the wars, tea was blended, coffee roasted, bread baked, bacon smoked and stationery printed, and in 1939 the Naafi sold £2 million of food and drink across the counters of its canteens, thus contributing to the welfare and comfort of the troops everywhere. On the outbreak of war contingency plans were drawn up to provide entertainment as well as nourishment, and the task of forming a special division for this purpose was turned over to theatre producer Basil Dean.

As we know from Shakespeare, some men are born great, some achieve greatness, and some have greatness thrust upon them. Fortunately the gods had given Dean, that rather taciturn magus of the British theatre, a formidable energy and unflagging determination; and he had already achieved a measure of greatness in World War I when he first conceived the idea of special troop shows for the soldiers fighting in France. He realised in 1939 that the Naafi connection was essential; they could supply the necessary finance and he could supply himself and whatever was required in the way of variety, drama or music.

Even before Munich he knew he was going to need a little help from his friends, and he had discussed his ideas with Owen Nares, Godfrey Tearle and the charmingly caustic Leslie Henson. They agreed to help initially, without knowing they were pledging themselves to a scheme where the top rate of pay, no matter how dazzling the star, would be a mere £10 a week.

Dean reported to the Naafi at Kennington Lane on Monday morning, 4 September, and he was given a cramped office with a desk and a telephone, but without even a typewriter for his secretary. He was sitting uneasily at his desk one morning during the first week of war, like a man adrift on a raft searching the horizon for help, and wondering how he was going to cope with his formidable job, when the phone rang.

It was his old friend Bill Abingdon, the stage director at the Theatre Royal and he had an idea: 'Would Dean like to take over Drury Lane as "temporary headquarters" for his new organisation?'

The same afternoon the chief executive of Entertainments National Service Association (ENSA) was ensconced in the plush comfort of the board room, planning to put into action: 'the voluntary mobilisation', as he termed it, 'of all branches of the profession for the provision of entertainment for the armed forces and munition workers of a country at war'. ENSA was on its way with a flourish and Drury Lane was transformed into 'Fit-up Alley'.

Another war had to be fought before braces were worn
openly on the terrace at Monte Carlo
Accompanist Ivor Newton

'For some reason,' said theatre producer Basil Dean, brows
furrowing as his memory flickered back over the years, 'a
snobbish attitude towards ENSA rapidly developed among
prominent members of the profession despite the fine
example set by Gracie Fields, George Formby and Dame
Edith Evans.

'This went on long after the war, especially among unknown artistes, as though they were ashamed of such a
derogatory connection. This is surprising when you consider
that ENSA helped bring about a change in government
attitude which raised the status of the theatre.

'When I look back on the story of what ENSA accom-
plished I sometimes wonder how on earth we did it all.'

While the potential for making mistakes was unlimited,
even its harshest critics could scarcely deny that ENSA – and
services-sponsored units like the Army Welfare *Stars in
Battledress* and the RAF's *Gang Show* – did make it possible
for a vast range of entertainers to work for the first time in
front of critical audiences, and many new artistes were
introduced who might otherwise have never received
recognition.

For thousands of unknowns it meant struggling along in the face of harsh and often dangerous conditions as they tried to maintain some kind of morale in the best tradition of show business. Whatever their shortcomings, they were easy-going and courageous.

Singers became dancers; ballerinas learned how to act; actors turned comedians, and comics played Shakespeare; ham-fisted amateurs were transformed into first-class professionals, and professionals who had worked on the end of the pier eventually found themselves topping the bill in magnificent opera-houses in cities like Cairo and Milan.

On 11 September 1939 the Theatre Royal, Drury Lane, became the official ENSA headquarters and it was against a backdrop of discarded sets from Novello's last show, *The Dancing Years* that operations quickly developed. Desks, chairs, typewriters, telephones, filing cabinets were set up in the room once used by Mrs Siddons. Garrick's old dressing-room, normally occupied by the star of the show, became a store-room, and the *Twelfth Night* cake ceremony was cancelled—a legacy had been left in 1794 by actor Robert Baddeley (ancestor of sisters Angela and Hermione) to provide a cake each year for the players appearing at Drury Lane. With no show in production, the £3 bequest went to charity.

The first official ENSA concert was given at the Old Dene camp, just outside London, on Sunday, 10 September 1939 with Frances Day and Arthur Riscoe. A week later, Bea Lillie, Annette Mills and a new radio personality called Jack Warner entertained the Royal Army Service Corps at Hurlingham Club.

Basil Dean soon established his committees, the largest being the variety section headed by Will Hay and ventrilo-quist Fred Russell (father of Val Parnell); Godfrey Tearle was given the job of setting up a drama division, Jack Hylton supplied dance bands and Harold Holt formed a classical concert group. Leslie Henson, whose casting vote had given the organisation its title, opened the first overseas department, working in it for a couple of weeks until boredom sent him to France to entertain the British Expeditionary Forces.

Lilian Braithwaite, with the help of Dame Sybil Thorndike, made herself responsible for running military hospital shows, and listened patiently to the complaints of small concert parties about the hardships involved in travelling miles out of London simply to play to meagre audiences of army doctors, medical orderlies and unmarried members of the ATS who thought they were pregnant (later on, this was the most common cause of the early release of numbers of the women's Auxiliary Territorial Service).

In the early days, ENSA's activities were favourably reported in the Press and some West-End stars descended on the Lane; perhaps scenting personal publicity, they offered to lend at least an air of distinction to the organisation. Among them, jostling to jump aboard the wagon, was the actor-manager Sir Seymour Hicks who had played for the troops in World War I, and was anticipating escorting a galaxy of stars to entertain the Guards at Buckingham Palace.

Dean would possibly have preferred despatching him to The Brigade of Gurkhas at Katmandu, but instead he ushered him into the room at the end of the main foyer – where Sheridan had worked on his *School for Scandal* – and appointed him ENSA's first controller, an honorary appointment involving a Mercator map of the British Isles and a small box of coloured pins to signify the location of each entertainment unit. He then went back to his own office and planned the first consignment of artistes for France.

According to Elsie Winsor, leading lady with one of the original seaside shows, *Hello Happiness* – and in the nature of these things, wife of the proprietor Reg Lever—ENSA 'was a proper *Dad's Army* set-up from the word go. We'd been playing a split week at Cambridge when Dean asked us if we could take the show overseas and it was all very exciting the first weeks, especially when Reg was called to the routing office after the dress rehearsal and handed a sealed envelope with instructions not to open it until we were well away from the Lane.

'Naturally we thought it would say Calais, and we were halfway to Dover before Reg realised it should have been Catterick. So we had to turn back and head north and when we got there, not a soul in sight, so we drove around for an hour until we found an empty hut with a bare stage and a few rows of benches.

'Some soldiers appeared and we were giving them a full-dress performance when a corporal came round and told us we were in the wrong place. There were 2,000 Royal Signals recruits waiting for us in the garrison theatre down the road. We cut the show short and ran out dressed in our costumes to start all over again for an audience who'd been sitting waiting for us over two hours.

'That's what I remember, the lack of planning, the blunders and the confusion and secret orders that didn't mean a thing. Of course it was even worse in France.'

And yet Reg Lever, his good lady and the rest of the cast of *Hello Happiness* stayed with ENSA until the war ended, taking the rough with the smooth and entertaining troops in all sorts of places and under all kinds of conditions.

Liverpool-born comedienne Avril Angers went to France with *Out of the Blue* and was nearly left out in the cold.

'I caught German measles at Arras – talk about germ warfare – and the company moved on; they left me hiding in a hotel bedroom with a packet of digestive biscuits, terrified in case I was dragged off to some strange French hospital.

'The company manager told me to tell anyone who came to the door that I was merely a little *sur le temps*, under the weather. Fortunately being young and healthy then, as well as incredibly lovely, I soon recovered and caught up with *Out of the Blue* on their way into Laon.'

An army convoy travelling towards the Belgian border in the first winter of the war saw a civilian car bogged down in the mud just outside Metz. As the leading 3-ton truck pulled up the soldiers in the back saw a familiar face.

'Hey up!' shouted a corporal, 'it's our Gracie!'

And it was Gracie Fields with her gaiety and humour in the broad down-to-earth idiom of Rochdale; that voice of startling clarity and irresistible quality. They crowded round to give her a welcome and a soldier said, as they always did, 'Sing us a song, Gracie.'

She threw her hat to Monty Banks in the front seat of the car, stood on the running-board and sang 'Sally' unaccompanied to soldiers perched on top of tanks and on the sides of Bren-gun carriers.

Gracie recalls: 'Most of the boys were like old friends. They'd seen me on the halls or heard me on the radio and I suppose I was part of the life they left behind. The songs I sang, "When I Grow Too Old To Dream" and "The Isle of Capri" and "Little Old Lady" were the ones they'd whistled on the way to work, and when they heard them again in France they were back home again for a little while.

'We went on to play Douai and Arras, and then did a concert for the RAF at Rheims. Then as soon as we got back to London Basil Dean arranged a tour right across Canada and the States to raise money for the Navy League.' She raised £170,000 on that first tour and £300,000 on a second one. In England she gave concerts in camps, factories and munition works. For her first performance back at Rochdale, Ivor Newton was the accompanist.

'It was a hectic six weeks,' he said, 'and I wouldn't have missed it for the world. ENSA was getting so many demands for Gracie from all over the country we felt Churchill's slogan should have been changed to "Give us Gracie and we'll finish the job!" Her energy was incredible, and unlike singers I normally worked with, the idea of saving or nursing her voice never occurred to her. It was exciting to accompany her and impossible to be indifferent to the genuine love and affection she commanded. Anyone could talk to her anywhere, and she was "Gracie" to them all, friends, strangers, fans; it didn't make any difference.'

Bandleader Joe Loss, eyes misting over, also recalls his time in wartime France. 'I know it's hard to believe, but I still get letters from fellows who were in the BEF in France when we worked there. We did concerts wherever there were troops, and I can tell you there was no shortage of entertainment. It was surprising how many top stars went across; two I remember seeing at the headquarters in Arras were Billy Cotton and Jack Buchanan.

'I told Jack Hylton just before we left London that the only thing I was short of was a good comedian, and he said he'd recently auditioned a boy who would be ideal, a cockney with all the makings of a future Max Miller. It was Charlie Chester so he came with us and we had a great show and could play anything up to three hours.'

One date Joe Loss played before he sailed to France was at Chelsea Barracks with a young vocalist who became the 'Sweetheart of the Forces' as the result of a *Daily Express* poll naming her as the most popular singer on the radio. A pretty girl may have been like a melody, but the BBC found that Vera Lynn – a plumber's daughter from East Ham – had a voice that transcended mere good looks. When she sang 'We'll Meet Again' she formulated all the sentiment and hopes of a country at war; in 'Wishing Will Make It So' she encouraged servicemen, their families and girl friends to think about the good times ahead 'when all the boys came back again' and her weekly broadcast brought mail by the sackful from lonely units, men overseas and men at sea in reply to her messages from the girls back home.

Jack Buchanan returned from France to tour army units in the home counties with Elsie Randolph and that large and jocund genius Fred Emney. Elsie Randolph remembers how appreciative the audiences were although 'conditions were crude. We sometimes did three shows a night and it was difficult for the girls in that very cold winter. They had to undress and change into costumes with no proper dressing-rooms and dance on rickety, makeshift stages. Quite often we had to dash across freezing fields of mud, all dolled up in our finery to reach the theatre. I always think of a soprano trying to sing "Your Tiny Hand is Frozen" in a Nissen hut with no heating of any kind in the middle of the coldest December in living memory. But if it was hard, it was also exhilarating for us after all the stuffy theatres we'd played before the war started.

'Then Basil Dean came along and put the boot in. He said that unless we became an official ENSA party he would have to clamp down on us. This would have meant all of us working for £10 a week and Jack didn't want to know. He told Dean we wouldn't do it; if we were going to work for nothing, we wouldn't need any help from ENSA.

'It ended up with a blazing row and the end of any connection with Drury Lane. After that we worked under our own steam.'

Fred Emney went into a show called *All Clear* which opened at the Queen's Theatre (with Bea Lillie, Adele Dixon and Bobby Howes) just before Christmas, making his first entrance complete with monocle and cigar dressed as a monstrous barrage balloon. It was during the run of the show that Bea Lillie's son, Bobby Peel, brought a fellow midshipman round to meet Fred, introducing him as Philip of Greece. Fred took them both out to supper at Ciro's and was delighted to find the young officer had a keen sense of humour. It was the beginning of a friendship with the Duke of Edinburgh that has lasted over the years.

As the activities of ENSA became more widespread and the great achievement of Basil Dean started to flower, Jack Payne (the leader of the BBC's first dance-band in the Savoy Hill days) came back from France. He was full of indignation and ready to give ENSA a sharp rap over the knuckles for its inefficiency.

'In all my experience,' Payne told reporters, 'I have never known such confusion. There wasn't a soul to meet us at Calais and we were kept hanging about the docks for well over six hours in the freezing cold. Twice poor Gracie Fields had to hold the fort for me because there was no transport, and when it did arrive it was usually an army truck. I do think it's a hell of a way to treat a top-class band.'

Didn't Payne complain to anyone?

'I certainly did. After being delayed half-a-dozen times I stormed on to the stage at Amiens in exasperation and told the audience what I thought about it.'

No doubt expecting the familiar strains of 'Say It With Music', they sat back and marvelled at the devastatingly direct nature of his accusations.

'And what,' asked the Press, 'was Mr Payne's solution to the problem?'

'Sack the bloody lot!'

Columns of criticism in the papers caused ENSA, in a bid to prevent further bad publicity, to add a clause to the contracts forbidding all artistes to give unauthorised interviews to the Press. However, facing the prospect of endless disputes, it was naïve of Dean to expect individualistic performers to accept restraints, war or no war. Egos have always flourished in the hothouse soil of the theatre, and self-absorption is an occupational disease.

Contending with a mounting tide of personal criticism, Dean explained that 'ENSA is decidedly not a one-man show . . . the ideas of many people have gone into the making of it'.

The editor of *World Review* alleged that '[ENSA] was largely a confraternity of fifth-rate artistes'. Dean replied that 'it does little justice either to the stars or lesser people whose bright and cheerful performances mean as much to the troops as the more publicised efforts of their peers'.

Ever aware that the defects of great men are the consolation of little men, Dean pointed out that ENSA was conducting the largest entertainment business in the world and was therefore able to stand up to a good deal of criticism. Privately he wondered whether the knocks were designed to improve matters or if they were inspired by spiteful self-interest.

Dean didn't know it at the time but the criticism from the Press was but a zephyr compared to the roaring hurricanes ahead. But as the increasing complexities of his job became more apparent he realised, at the end of 1939, that a good administrator was urgently required at Drury Lane.

He discussed things with Jack Hylton who suggested Charles Munyard, an experienced man of the theatre who had been with Paramount Theatres for some years before joining the Hylton office as assistant manager. Charlie Munyard remained with ENSA all during the war, organising the Lease-Lend Department – a pool of unattached artistes who could be sent anywhere as replacements or to complete a company – and 'after I straightened that lot out I took over the Overseas Section with Pete Collins'.

The Christmas of 1939 was at least quiet, with the British Expeditionary Forces (BEF) dug-in along the Franco–Belgian border and the French Army keeping a close watch on the Maginot Line. The king spoke on the radio as usual at 3 pm on Christmas Day; and in the evening, by the firelight glow, Britain sat and listened to a concert, starring Gracie Fields, relayed from the Western Front. The day finished with a broadcast from a West-End cabaret featuring Cyril Fletcher with Freddie Ballerini's orchestra.

People who could afford a night out in London celebrated the holiday dancing at Rectors to Jack Jackson's band or at the Kit Kat Club where Teddy Joyce supplied the music. Harry Roy was resident band leader at the Café Anglais, and Carroll Gibbons reopened at the Savoy Hotel with an orchestra that included Paul Fenouhlet, who later went into the RAF and formed the famous 'Sky Rockets' dance band.

Commercial theatres were doing good business, but with the exception of a revue at the Palladium, *The Little Dog Laughed* with Flanagan and Allen, most of the productions were either revivals or tepid comedies.

The Piccadilly Theatre revived *The Corn Is Green* with

Sybil Thorndike. 'I had finished filming *The Stars Look Down* two days before the war was declared,' said Emlyn Williams, 'and the next picture was naturally postponed so I immediately began work for the War Office, deciphering telegrams at Wormwood Scrubs, until the authorities decided I might be more useful keeping fifty people in work by taking *The Corn Is Green* on tour at the end of the London run.'

A comedy, *Somewhere in England*, was at the Lyric with Marie Lohr and Will Hay in the main roles; Gillie Potter carried on with *Gaieties de Montmartre* at the Prince of Wales, and the 128th edition of *Revudeville* opened at the Windmill Theatre. Tom Walls's own play, *His Majesty's Guest,* closed after only a short run of fifty-three performances, the same week Joan Hickson opened in *As You Are.*

Me and My Girl went back into the Victoria Palace and The Old Vic company played the Opera House, Manchester, with Marie Ney, Constance Cummings and Robert Donat.

Constance Cummings remembers: 'We had excellent houses wherever we played, and most of them seemed to be young people who had only seen Robert Donat in films before. They used to wait outside the stage-door for hours, in the freezing winter, just to take a closer look at him.

'Naturally when war broke out, one felt that the bottom had dropped out of one's world. I had a fierce argument with Leslie Banks; he had been badly wounded in World War I and because of it he insisted that anything in the world was better than war, but I was sure we did the right thing. I've always been strongly aware of the dangers of fascism and I believed we were right to fight it; I still do. Of course the theatre in those days was very divided, but I've always held the view that people should never be suppressed by force.'

Searching for a way of spreading a little happiness over the Christmas season, The Earl and Countess of Pembroke decided to do their wartime bit by presenting a pantomime for some of the RAF stationed in the immediate vicinity of their *Upstairs, Downstairs* demesne in Wiltshire.

Heil Cinderella was specially written by Cecil Beaton and John Sutro, and it numbered no less than eight peers, nine peeresses and one bishop on its list of patrons. The costumes were supplied 'by London's most exclusive dressmaker'— who was nameless—and there was glamour of a kind in the shape of a line-up of bucolic debutantes.

Lady Juliet Duff, a stunning six-footer, made a stylish Queen and the formidable Lady Mayor, Miss Edith Olivier, radiated benevolent menace as the Wicked Witch. Cecil Beaton was a glossy Ugly Sister in full drag, heavily sequinned and enveloped in a cloud of tulle; when he wasn't upstaging the Witch he was blatantly flashing his jewel-studded stirrup cup at Buttons, played by the Honourable David Herbert.

Prince Charming (Lady Drummond-Hay) closed the show, declining a flagon of mulled wine as she carefully articulated her final lines:

> I thank you but I have a flask
> I always carry in my mask;
> Why wear a thing that makes you throttle,
> If you can't use it to hold a bottle?

So pleased was the Earl with his success as an impresario he sent round two whole cases of vintage champagne to the cast—a gesture he doubtless regretted some months later when German soldiers trampled all over the French vineyards.

There was a hogshead of ale for the audience who all joined in a chorus of 'Bless 'Em All' with the gentry and toasted the nobs of old England before marching cheerfully through thick snowdrifts back to the primitive comfort of their billets. None of the RAF men realised they had been watching a museum piece left over from an age that ended on a Sunday morning in September 1939.

The winning of Waterloo has been attributed to some odd
playing fields but never I think to the stage of the
Theatre Royal, Drury Lane

Ivor Brown, 1940

'In those days,' said Pat Kirkwood, 'stardom meant coming
offstage, going home to mother and grilling yourself a chop.'

She was recalling the eighteen-year-old unknown from
Manchester who appeared in *Black Velvet* at the London
Hippodrome and made headlines as 'Britain's first wartime
stage star ... with a personality as inescapable as sheet light-
ning and a voice vibrant as a dynamo and as soft as Deanna
Durbin's.'

Black Velvet, the hit show of 1940, starring Vic Oliver,
was a spectacular revue presented by the outstanding show
business figure of World War II, George Black. Combining
an instinct for showmanship with a keen sense of business,
he was an arbiter of public taste and right from the beginning
of his long association with Moss Empires he brought about
a revival of interest in light entertainment.

Pat Kirkwood began her career at the age of fourteen,
singing songs on the BBC's *Children's Hour* accompanied
by pianist Violet Carson (better known today as 'Ena
Sharples' of *Coronation Street*). She takes up the story: 'Before
Black Velvet I toured the provinces and the nearest I got to

the West End was a week at the Metropolitan, Edgware Road, singing songs like "The Touch of Your Lips" and "Chapel in the Moonlight", and I was lucky enough to be a hit. On the Thursday night the microphone wasn't working so I stepped forward, told the audience and sang without it. Prince Littler was in front and on the strength of that he booked me for pantomime at Cardiff. Cast as the principal girl I was awful, and even though he'd signed me for a three-year option Littler wanted to let me go. Fortunately his wife [Nora Delaney] said: "Don't do that, this girl's got talent but she should be playing principal boy."

'So he put me into *Cinderella* as Dandini with Madge Elliott and Stanley Lupino at the Prince's Theatre. I was scared stiff on the first morning and we were rehearsing in the stalls bar when mother appeared, tripped down the stairs and fell straight into Stanley Lupino's arms. I simply wanted to die, there and then.'

Pat survived and went back on the road again and was playing the Grand Theatre, Bolton when her agent Don Ross rang to say she had to get back to London: George Black was holding auditions at the Palladium for a new show. Pat recalls: 'I didn't even have a change of costume with me but I travelled all night to be there in time. I never told anyone then, not even mother, how nervous I used to get. I was always in a dreadful state on Monday afternoons after the band call, and I'd usually go and sit in a cinema although I never saw the film, I was so ill with nerves. Once the first night was over I felt much better.

'Anyway I got to the Palladium clutching my make-up box and band parts and Jack Hylton took one look at them and said, "I can't play these bloody things! They'll have to be recopied."

'Feeling terrible I crept into the nearest dressing-room and started slapping on greasepaint until a call-boy came and shouted: "You're on!" I went on stage and sang my song, thinking to myself that I hadn't a hope of getting the part and I was surprised when I got a round of applause from all the other acts sitting in the stalls.

'I was back in the dressing-room taking off the make-up when Hylton walked in. "You've got it all, little girl," he said, "the West End show *and* we're putting you in a film with Arthur Askey." That was *Band Waggon*, but after it finished there was nothing except an offer from Joe Loss to sing with his band. I went back on tour and did a little radio to help the money situation and finally George Black sent for me.'

After the first night she got all the usual invitations to parties but turned them all down and hurried back home to the traditional grilled chop. Early the next morning, George Black's son Alfred was on the telephone asking if she'd seen the papers.

Pat rushed out to buy them all and got so tired reading them she fell asleep again.

'By eleven o'clock, the people and flowers and champagne started arriving and no one took any notice of me, so I quietly left the flat and walked all the way to the theatre. I stood on the corner of Cranbourne Street looking up at my name over the Hippodrome and I didn't feel anything at all.

'Naturally every performer dreams of seeing their name in lights and I don't think I was any exception, but it was a few years before that happened. The blackout put paid to that.

'Although it was a strange time to be growing up, especially in the theatre, we could at least claim the unique experience of acting and dancing during bombing raids and singing "It's a Lovely Day Tomorrow" while we wondered if we'd manage to survive the night. And it was difficult if you were a girl; clothes, such as they were, on the ration and no decent shoes or stockings, just at the age when these things seemed terribly important. And on top of everything else, most of the boys of the same age were all away in the forces.

'But in spite of everything, there was something exciting

about being part of it. There was a feeling for life none of us will ever forget. Most of us sensed it and we were more alive then than at any other time in our lives.

'People generally seemed to be at their best and we were all trying to make a small contribution to what we hoped would be a better world. I'm grateful for having lived through those years.'

Someone else hoping to make his contribution to a better world was the 'Discovery King', Carroll Levis, who arrived back unexpectedly in London in January 1940.

The day after war was declared he suddenly made up his mind to visit his old mother back in Vancouver and, checking his bank account and cancelling all contracts, he paid off his discoveries and saw his large car safely loaded aboard 'The Duchess of Atholl' at Liverpool, bound for Canada.

The newspapers, having noted his precipitate departure, were curious about his return. Had it anything to do with the fact that there'd been no bombing as yet? Levis airily dismissed all questions, explaining he had only gone home to set up a trust fund for momma.

'She's a dear old lady but not a good business woman. Now I'm back in business again and I've got some great ideas for the boys. I hope to take a company over to France and then maybe put on a show in London.'

No one was more surprised to see him again than his former manager, Leonard Urry. He had decided to carry on with a 'Discoveries' tour after his boss went home and had the publicity billing corrected to read 'Carroll Levis's BBC Discoveries, compered by Leonard Urry, discoverer of Carroll Levis', until an outraged cable from his master in Canada forced the promoters to change it to 'Leonard Urry, discoverer of Carroll Levis, presents BBC Discoveries'. The tour continued to do well and the acts were paid from £4 a week for singles and up to £20 for double acts, plus bonuses.

It was Urry who later presented a sixteen-year-old singer from Dulwich 'likely to lift the crooning art out of the rut'.

The name of their particular discovery was Anne Shelton.

Carroll Levis never managed to stage his show in London during the war. A highly successful entrepreneur in the late thirties, with earnings calculated at just under £250,000, his timing in 1940 was at fault.

According to Tolstoy, who had been a correspondent in the Crimean War, one of the chief attractions of military service lay in the long spells of compulsory idleness between battles; in the 'phoney war' it became an accepted fact of life that entertainment on a large scale was not only a major morale booster but the British fighting spirit could only be sustained in shelter, trench or factory if it was fortified with liberal doses of Arthur Askey's *Band Waggon*, Tommy Handley's *ITMA* and Jack Warner's *Garrison Theatre*.

Although previous battles might well have been won without the help of troop concerts, what had been for centuries a minor inconvenience fought by hardened professionals became by the end of 1940 a universal death struggle from which no home was safe. As a result there developed among servicemen and war workers, in fact the whole population whose familiar world had crumbled, a longing to rediscover if only for an hour or two a magic enclave where war faded into insignificance.

With this in mind the Pilgrim Trust made a grant of £25,000 for the purpose of keeping people in good heart 'by the practice and patronage of the Arts'. (The Trust had been founded in 1930 by the American banker, Edward Harkness, who left £2 million to be spent for the benefit of Britain in appreciation of the country's acceptance of the financial burdens of World War I.) Before the war it was used for social-welfare schemes, grants to cultural societies, and for the purchase of works of art.

A Committee for the Encouragement of Music and Arts, CEMA, was appointed by the Pilgrim Trust under the chairmanship of Lord Macmillan who was also chairman of the Trust. The principal work of organising was done by Mary Glasgow, formerly an Inspector of Schools, and the purpose of the Committee was to find work for the actors, musicians, singers and painters who had lost work as a result of the closure of theatres and halls when war began. Ivor Brown was a director of CEMA's theatrical activities in May 1940, and remained until June 1942 when he became editor of *The Observer*. The exact function of CEMA was undefined even when it became a Council in April 1940, but the statement that it set out 'to maintain the highest possible standard of the arts in wartime and to distribute them as widely as possible to those who ... were cut off from them' was summed up later by Ivor Brown as 'the Best for the Most'.

The first £25,000 soon went, mainly to individual artistes, and as soon as the news of CEMA's activities spread, appeals for money multiplied, particularly as the only stipulation was that anyone receiving aid made no profit. Life became much easier for out-of-work musicians who were sent to remote places and discovered new audiences with a genuine enthusiasm for classical music. Another development was the support of national orchestras which enabled them to carry out a number of extra concerts and keep their membership and traditions in being.

Smaller concerts were also presented in factories, until the Ministry of Labour ruled that the provision of entertainment for munition workers should be undertaken by ENSA, taking away part of CEMA's work in this territory. Consequently it was decided to find further scope for professional musicians by giving recitals in the churches, chapels and cathedrals of districts most affected by war.

At the beginning there was close rivalry between the two organisations, and the relationship between them was frequently confused. Although ENSA's activities sometimes coincided with CEMA's, its aims were more restricted and it was purely a wartime entertainment service, whereas CEMA provided opportunities for hearing good music and for the encouragement of the arts among all kinds of people under a permanent system of government aid which led to the eventual development of the Arts Council.

ENSA, underlining its separate function, published a bulletin listing its overseas achievements; thirty-one companies, a total of nearly 500 performers, had been sent to France and other places abroad.

At home there were thirty concert parties on tour; nearly 300 plays were produced and over 700 variety shows given, including hospital concerts. This didn't include the four-handed groups in small vans who travelled with a mini-piano to hold a hundred sing-songs every week, or the solo accordionists who went to searchlight batteries. And garrison theatres at larger bases had opened in sufficient numbers to enable the same play to tour for four months at a time.

Scottish actor Alex McCrindle, who had been working for Equity compiling a list of actors still available, was transferred to Drury Lane to open a Central Registry for ENSA in what had been the 'star' dressing-room:

'I remember standing in a great heap of letters from applicants thinking to myself that if I didn't get out of there soon I'd be lost to sight forever. Henry Oscar was rehearsing one of the first plays, *Eight Bells*, so I went and asked him if I could stage-manage it on tour.

'Most of those new garrison theatres we went to had one thing in common, none of them had any kind of heating backstage. *Eight Bells* was set on a ship stranded in the tropics so you can imagine what it was like for the cast, all dressed in light clothes, blue with cold and when they weren't speaking, their mouths clamped together to stop their teeth chattering. As they were supposed to be overcome by the heat of the blazing sun, the acting was magnificent.

'None of us realised it at the time but a young actor from Huddersfield who was in *Eight Bells* was soon to become a big star.'

This was James Mason, whose experience in repertory included a season at the Gate Theatre, Dublin, where he followed Orson Welles as guest actor. One of the first 'legitimate' actors engaged by ENSA, he toured the service units until he was able to make his way into films later on, starring in romantic costume pieces like *The Wicked Lady* and *The Man in Grey*.

It was suggested in 1940 that professional performers of military age should be exempted from call-up, but Basil Dean didn't agree; he felt they should do their bit just like any other worker, and as far as ENSA was concerned there were over 5,000 artistes available so he wasn't experiencing any shortage. His only difficulty was turning unsuitable applicants away.

But other people were not too happy at some of ENSA's activities. Condemning stage nudity in a letter published in the spring, the vicar of St Saviour's Church, Chelsea, wondered whether the country was worthy of victory when he considered the obscenity and indecency seen in a number of London theatres: 'And I heard recently of a concert given to our troops in France which was so disgusting some nurses walked out in the middle of it. Although the authorities have now decided to take immediate steps to cleanse theatres and cabarets, it seems it has to take a war to reach such a decision.'

Dean characteristically brushed aside such statements and told a London Press Club dinner that in his view stage nudity was simply a war neurosis. It was a licence, not a freedom, and it would soon pass. After all, what troops didn't like down-to-earth broad humour?

The RAF weren't all that pleased about it, according to former pilot Frank Tinsdale, who felt people were much more strait-laced in those days. 'While we were training at Cosford near Wolverhampton an ENSA company played *Love in a Mist*, and they added some lines obviously not in the original script. Perhaps they thought it might go over better with an RAF audience if they included a few smutty remarks and as I remember the play lent itself to them.

'However, even though our average age then was only eighteen, some of us began booing when the actors overdid it, and that had the desired effect. I'm sure today the sort of lines they added wouldn't even be noticed.'

The dance bands in those days were playing tunes made popular before the war like 'Ten Pretty Girls' and ''Neath the Spreading Chestnut Tree'; there were no songs like 'Tipperary' or Novello's 'Keep the Home Fires Burning', and servicemen seemed to prefer melodies that reminded them of home.

There wasn't a great deal of inspiration for songwriters; favourite names for girls in those days being Kay or Betty, Joy or Joan, none of them calculated to quicken a lyricist's heart with pleasure. Noel Gay wrote 'Run, Rabbit, Run' after hearing about a rabbit killed by a wayward practice bomb dropped on the Shetlands, and Jimmy Kennedy came up with 'We're Gonna Hang Out Our Washing on the Siegfried Line' after nights spent pacing up and down on sentry duty at an anti-aircraft site. American imports included 'The Umbrella Man', popularised by Bud Flanagan, and 'Franklin D. Roosevelt Jones'. A much-sung soldiers' ballad started life in the city of Prague as 'Pity of Love' – it got to America, where it was renamed 'The Beer Barrel Polka', and finally arrived in Britain as 'Roll Out the Barrel'.

George Formby, back from a visit to France in 1940, was touring naval bases in Scotland, still singing the songs that made him a star in his own outgoing style. He was called for military service, but the years staying at the top as Britain's highest-paid comedian had taken their toll and he failed the medical because of 'a nasal ailment and stiff toes'. Formby started out as an ordinary comic trying to follow his father's profession after failing as a jockey; but his wife Beryl must have seen some potential in his essential simplicity and high-pitched voice, and so she built him up, pulled him together, and pushed him to the top, even co-starring in his first film *Boots*, made in 1934 on a budget of less than £3,000.

By 1940 Formby was the most popular male star in British

films, topping the poll ahead of people like Robert Donat, Gracie Fields and Anna Neagle; he was listed fifth in an American box-office poll after Mickey Rooney, Deanna Durbin, Spencer Tracy and Jeanette MacDonald. Although George's wife provided the impetus, he also gave her a great deal. Every birthday there was a new Rolls Royce for her, his home near Blackpool was named 'Beryldene', and he christened his yacht 'Lady Beryl', so naturally people were surprised to hear about his engagement to a girl twenty years his junior soon after Beryl died. But the marriage never took place; George himself died before it could be arranged.

Meanwhile, in a rare moment of inspiration (and with anxious days about to begin) ENSA decided to stage a couple of 'summit' concerts in association with its French counter-part, *Théâtre aux Armées*. The first was presented at Drury Lane in the presence of the Duke and Duchess of Kent and the French ambassador, with Gracie Fields and Maurice Chevalier topping the bill, supported by Binnie Hale, Stanley Holloway and Richard Hearne; music was provided by Carroll Gibbons and Jack Hylton's band.

'Just before the concerts,' recalled Gracie Fields, 'Monty Banks and I had decided to get married. We also wanted to see my mother who was ill in California so we flew there from Canada and got married. On the second day of the honeymoon Basil Dean rang me from London to say he needed me to appear with Chevalier at Drury Lane and the Paris Opera House, to help promote goodwill between Britain and France.

'We came back straight away and did the concerts and as soon as they were finished I decided to tour around the BEF based in France. We didn't see London again until just before Dunkirk.'

It was reported from Paris that at the Opera House concert 'Mme Elsa Schiaperelli created a sensation, as always, with her perfectly straight dress topped by a little jacket with a rose-pink front, embroidered all over with many-coloured sequins, and pink satin gloves to match, similarly spangled. On her head she wore an astonishing turban, knotted high on top like an intensely elegant bathing cap.'

Richard Murdoch, in France with Arthur Askey on a brief ENSA tour, remembers working with Gracie Fields at concerts in Amiens and Lille. 'When she walked on the stage at Amiens she couldn't start her first song for a long time because of the great reception the troops gave her. It was the same wherever she played, they all loved her.

'When the tour finished I stayed on for a while as I'd never been in France before and it looked very much as though it might be the last time I'd see Paris for God knows how long. I certainly picked a fine time with the German army about to stroll through the Maginot Line.'

'I was very lucky,' continues Murdoch, 'because I worked a lot in the theatre all during the war; I didn't get paid for it but it kept me going. Every time I got a forty-eight hour pass Henry Hall would put me in one of his *Guest Nights* and they also released me for three weeks to make a film.'

Posted to the Air Ministry in London later in the war, he shared an office with Kenneth Horne (seconded from Balloon Command) and together they created the highly successful and long-running *Much-Binding-in-the-Marsh* radio series: 'Most of the scripts were written in the Royal Automobile Club in Pall Mall.'

Henry Oscar's daughter Doreen was touring France in April and May with an ENSA production of *Night Must Fall*, playing garrison theatres at Nantes, Boulogne, Calais, Amiens and Lille, and she also has vivid memories of Gracie Fields:

'I was at Lille when Gracie Fields arrived for a concert and of course the theatre was packed to the doors. Dickie Murdoch smuggled me into the wings so I could see her and it was a marvellous experience. She completely won them over in the first minutes of her act and the ovation at the end was the loudest I'd ever heard.'

The Sadler's Wells Ballet also saw something of the

European theatre of war. The company, with Margot Fonteyn, Moyra Fraser and Robert Helpmann, was on a goodwill tour of Holland under the auspices of the British Council and had just completed their fourth performance at Arnhem when the Germans invaded. Their bus, only hours in front of the panzers, reached the Hague safely and they sheltered in the British Legation through anxious days of bombing and street fighting.

Margot Fonteyn saw 'paratroopers dropping all round the town; and German residents began firing at the Dutch from their windows'. The company managed to get on the last boat out but had to leave the scenery, costumes, music and all personal belongings behind.

Ralph Reader, commissioned in the RAF, had taken his first *Gang Show* to France in October 1939, under the ENSA banner with 'four of the original Scout *Gang Show* chaps and Bill Sutton, former assistant stage-manager at Drury Lane'.

Bill Sutton also joined the air-force and worked with Reader until the end of the war, organising the official RAF Gang Shows in different parts of the world.

'In France', he said, 'we put on shows for the advanced striking force; I remember meeting the New Zealand air ace, "Cobber" Kain over there (he was killed on 11 June as the guns of the Maginot Line opened their heaviest shelling of the war), and we always found an excuse for a party. One night we were billeted in a hotel at Rheims.

'We didn't know it at the time but the Duke of Windsor was staying at the hotel and just as the party was getting under way a message came down to us in the lounge saying "Pipe down, His Royal Highness can't sleep." A message went straight back upstairs, "Compliments to His Royal Highness but His Majesty's Air Force will close the bar when they're good and ready." Then we went on with the party.'

The show was well received at all the RAF stations and in June 1940 'just got out of France by the skin of its teeth, with the German army at its heels'.

During the last week in May all entertainments for the troops in France, with the exception of cinema shows, were 'temporarily suspended', and over 200 ENSA personnel arrived back in London; among them was Will Hay who had experienced several air-raids while appearing for the BEF near the Belgian border.

The last ENSA company out of France, 'The Strolling Players', came back in a troopship and the cast of the play *While Parents Sleep* were evacuated with the army from Dunkirk; Mai Bacon returned unscathed, on a hospital ship, and went straight into rehearsal for a new show, *Nuts and Mai*. One of the last artistes out of Le Havre was Basil Dean's wife, actress Victoria Hopper.

Jack DeManio was in the BEF as a lieutenant with Peter's force, 7th Royal Sussex Regiment. Most of his battalion were trapped in a train bombed by enemy aircraft outside Amiens:

'Because it was supposed to be a second-line battalion it hadn't had much training and carried very few weapons. They had no anti-tank guns, the men with arms had the wrong ammunition and the officers didn't even have service revolvers. On top of the bombing they were caught in the middle of a tank battle, so that out of a whole battalion numbering 800, only five officers and 250 men got back to England; the rest were either killed or taken prisoner.

'I was lucky I wasn't on the train myself. I'd been sent on to Rouen with the company sergeant-major and an advance party, and in the end it was our job to gather the remnants together to try and get them back safely. We reported to the base where the men were to pick up their kits which were laid out along the ground with each soldier marching along the company lines to stand next to his own kit. There were all these fearful gaps where kits were laid out with no one standing alongside, and I just sat on the step of a burnt-out truck, looking at all the empty spaces. One soldier standing there and nothing either side of him for ten or fifteen yards; one man only occupied half a yard and there were so many more spaces than soldiers. It still upsets me to think about it.'

He eventually managed to get back: 'not the common way through Dunkirk but by a much more chic route through Cherbourg. Back in England I was disgusted to find we were expected to "double" everywhere. We had done so much running in France, you'd have thought they might have left us alone for a while.'

The company sergeant-major was given a Distinguished Conduct Medal and three officers were awarded the Military Cross. Jack DeManio was one of them.

Actress Freda Gaye (who edited Pitman's *Who's Who in the Theatre* for a number of years after the war) was in a theatre festival at Canterbury during May: 'I had been given leave of absence for the four weeks by the repertory company at Bexhill, but when France fell the project was cancelled. I remember dissolving in tears during Churchill's speech, although all I wrote in my diary was "Belgium and France invaded. Opening tonight in *The Dominant Sex*."

'I was back at Bexhill at the end of the month, at the time of Dunkirk. We could hear the guns across the Channel and it seemed such a strange contrast in that blazingly still summer. An absolutely cloudless sky, and yet a sense of impending disaster overshadowing everything. We had a house on the beach at the time and I always look back on it as the last of the good summers, the end of the golden days. From then on it was all acute anxiety and frenzied activity. France had fallen, the Germans were about to invade us, and it seemed we had lost the war, although there wasn't a soul in Britain prepared to believe it.'

By 15 June 1940 all ENSA's staff were safely back from France and the hundred officers and men of 'Naafi-Efi' – the Expeditionary Forces Institute – who paraded on the stage of the Theatre Royal the following morning were the military section of ENSA; carpenters, electricians, drivers and commanders who had been working not only behind the scenes but behind the lines as well. The last three troop shows were given in France a few hours before the Germans arrived, and the ENSA men were forced to make a run for it, covering a journey of 150 miles by night without leaving a scrap of equipment behind. A projectionist was screening a film in the town of Vitry-le-François as the first enemy tank rolled into the main street. He stopped the show abruptly and managed to escape.

The only casualties reported were one lieutenant killed in an air-raid and a corporal driver shot dead at the wheel of a lorry.

Among the returned officers, most of whom had worked in the theatre before the war, was Captain Lance Fairfax, well known in musicals of the thirties. A New Zealander, he was in *The Tivoli Follies* in Sydney in 1921, and came to London to make his début on *Bow Bells*. He toured in *Waltzes from Vienna*, and was in *Music in the Air* at His Majesty's Theatre for C. B. Cochran. Before opening an agency in the fifties he appeared in concerts and worked for the BBC. He died in January 1974 aged seventy-three, leaving a widow, Karen Greer, and a daughter, Jenny.

With two million soldiers under arms in Britain at the beginning of July, with little to do except wait for the combined forces of Germany and Italy to descend on them, ENSA shows were in greater demand than ever.

At Drury Lane, seventy people a day were auditioned and according to a spokesman, 'Talent, not sex-appeal, was wanted. The troops want to be amused, not vamped.' All-women concert parties and 'revuettes' were formed, the first two named *Out of the Basket* and *All Women*. With the rapid expansion of the variety division, the number of auditions for artistes anxious to offer their services were stepped up, and with more than 100,000 French soldiers billeted in temporary camps in the south, arrangements were made for the supply of French films.

ENSA began a twice-weekly broadcast on both the Home and Forces programmes, *Break for Music*, and John Gielgud, Mary Ellis, Henry Oscar and Geraldo and his Orchestra were in the first transmission with Clive Brook as guest compère. Geraldo suggested that Basil Dean might select a signature tune for the broadcasts and he picked Noel Gay's 'Let the People Sing', 'because of its bright beat and optimism'. It opened the shows for the next six years.

Ernest Bevin (Minister of Labour in the coalition government) opened a radio show called *Between Shifts*, especially organised for munition workers. Two thousand of them filled the canteen to be entertained by Will Fyffe and soprano Joan Cross.

The concert was introduced by Basil Dean who told the audience: 'Wherever needed we shall send you entertainment and if the work is interrupted from the skies, we will carry our songs with you below ground.'

'That's right,' agreed Bevin, 'let the people sing, particularly munition workers.' He turned to the workers.

'Well, mates,' he said, 'I believe that as well as saying "Go to it", we should also "Sing with it" and in fact we've organised a quartet in the government to make this scheme work. As well as myself, there's Lord Beaverbrook, Herbert Morrison and A. V. Alexander and we want to brighten things up a bit for you. The more you do, the quicker we'll get this wretched job over and done with.'

The Times reported the approval of the Ministry of Labour for the concerts and voiced its anxiety on the needs 'of that increasingly large public to whom a Bach concerto or a Tchaikovsky symphony was the most inspiring experience.

'Must the great orchestras of the country be left to make periodic appeals to charity and depend for their existence on the sympathetic enterprises of music halls? Other countries, including enemy countries, have found a satisfactory answer to the question. Surely it isn't beyond Britain's capacity to find its own?'

CEMA agreed to collaborate with ENSA on a better type of concert for factories, presenting music 'of the highest concert-hall standard'; commercial managers expressed fears that these free shows were competing unfairly with their theatres. ENSA pointed out that the shows couldn't possibly be in competition as they were only taking place at lunchtime. They also stated that arrangements had been made for The Performing Rights Society to accept special rates for music provided by all their artistes. Any broadcasting fees earned by these artistes were distributed among theatrical and musical charities.

In the months before the evacuation from Dunkirk, theatres in London and major provincial towns were doing excellent business; no doubt people were bored with waiting on events and perhaps they needed to get as much distraction and pleasure while the going was still comparatively good. And with seaside resorts closed to summer visitors, there was more money to spend in cities as higher wages for war workers meant that they could spend more on relaxation.

Leslie Grade's *West End Varieties* was playing in three different music-halls in London; his brother, up-and-coming agent Bernard Delfont, continued to be active booking artistes as the sole agent for Mecca Dance Halls, as well as supplying acts for variety theatres. His agency had done well since it opened in 1937, and with the help of general manager Arthur Crocker it had launched several road shows, revivals of earlier West-End musical successes.

John Gielgud offered his services to ENSA and an elderly small-part actress, hearing that he was thinking about touring Chekhov for the troops, said to a friend, 'Well dear, I always thought Chekhov's a right bastard to play and I don't think the boys'll like it very much; but of course I'm a bit common. When you come to think of it, though, some of the boys are a bit common too, aren't they?'

Gielgud set her mind at rest. He took out Noel Coward's *Fumed Oak* with Bea Lillie, and they packed every garrison theatre they visited.

When he reopened the Old Vic earlier in 1940 with *King Lear*, the response of the public had been very good and until the fall of France, when the war swept to the shores of Britain, every performance had played to capacity ensuring enough money to carry on until July. In normal times his second production, *The Tempest*, designed by Oliver Messel, would have been a great attraction, but after Dunkirk there was a general desire to stay home and dig for victory or go out and drill with the newly formed Home Guard.

At the end of June only one play, *Rebecca*, was still running in London and revues had been reduced to a handful.

BBC radio, while it found work for some entertainers, didn't help fill theatres and as at any time of crisis or expectancy the lure of the nine o'clock news was strong. Thousands of Londoners who might normally have stayed in town and gone to a show at night, went straight home to the suburbs.

Basil Dean, getting a little of his own back, was openly critical about the BBC, particularly their attitude to the broadcasts from Germany of 'Lord Haw-Haw' (who was, of course, William Joyce, the broadcaster of Nazi propaganda in English from Germany during the war. Captured in 1945, he was tried for treason and executed.)

'The whole of the Corporation', said Dean, 'were suffering from mental rickets and they didn't realise the nation's needs. They should *jam* Lord Haw-Haw, not build him up; the man was a danger and a peril. And another thing, it's time they realised the days of the old school tie are dead and gone. Now they're only liable to choke on it.'

There were only 350 Equity members working in London out of a total of 5,000, and with no musicals running, hundreds of chorus-girls were out of work. The Adelphi and Strand theatres were converted into clubs for Australian and New Zealand soldiers then landing in England; the Garrick and the Aldwych were up for sale.

A new arrival on the scene, the small theatre club, flourished in spite of the threat of air-raids. People preferred to gather in converted rooms and small halls rather than in spacious theatres; a double attraction being the moderate charge for admission and the atmosphere of friendly intimacy. The public were also able to see plays of distinction rather than tired revivals and routine 'escapist' shows. The Torch, Gate, Unity and Neighbourhood theatres, operating on small capital and low-cost production, signposted the way to the cheaper, more flexible and elemental theatre now thriving in London and other cities.

The Neighbourhood Theatre opened in June and made an immediate impact with *Thunder Rock* (by American writer Robert Ardrey), a play linking the living and the dead, drawing lessons from the past to bear on the present, to make a strong argument against isolation whether of the individual or the state. It was later filmed by Roy Boulting, who had been acclaimed for his earlier pictures, *Desert Victory* and *Burma Victory*, and his brother John.

Michael Redgrave starred in the film as the man who, disgusted by human folly and stupidity, seeks refuge on a lighthouse rock.

The London Gate Theatre tried to maintain its contacts in spite of censorship with foreign writers of distinction, and the Shakespeare Festival was again presented in its pastoral setting at the Memorial Theatre at Stratford-upon-Avon. There, only the fleecy vapour-trails of fighter aircraft high in the blue sky could create a fusion of the past and present.

While the war should have given a new impetus to the film industry, feature-film output in 1940 fell to a mere fifty-six pictures and the Ministry of Information, recognising the need to record the historic events taking place, brought together a group of documentary film makers under Sir Kenneth (now Lord) Clark, the director of the National Gallery from 1934–45. He was succeeded by Jack Beddington, a man with an understanding of the aims of documentary films; he was responsible for the MOI Films Division throughout the war.

Seymour Hicks voiced his disgust in the newspapers about those British actors 'who had rushed to America to escape military service' and he was concerned about the future of those he understood were making a new film there called *Gone With the Wind Up* and those others so gallantly facing the full glare of the footlights in New York.

He felt the British public should help put an end to this scandal 'by writing to any young star they suspected of shirking wartime responsibilities asking if he intended to come home, and if not, why not? If the reply was unsatisfactory then boycott the young bounder's picture. That was the only way to deal with him.'

A few months later, during the worst of the blitz, Sir Seymour decided to accept engagements in South Africa.

British stage and film actors in the USA were told they should return to Britain if they were liable for military service; among those in Hollywood were Patric Knowles, Richard Greene, Louis Hayward, Robert Coote and Hughie Green – Coote and Green went to Canada and joined the RCAF.

The popularity of some British stars suffered as a result of their absence in Hollywood, and the studios talked about a reduction in salary because of the loss of income abroad. The British colony in the film capital were most upset by the suggestion that they were 'deserters'.

Greer Garson, who had earned £4 a week in the Birmingham Repertory Theatre, decided she should go back. She went to the British Consul in Los Angeles who asked her what she intended to do. 'I could drive an ambulance or even run a soup kitchen,' she told him. He said she'd be much more useful making films and she heard later that according to Winston Churchill, one film like *Mrs Miniver* was more effective than a whole flotilla of destroyers.

Anna Neagle and Laurence Olivier had sent back £175,000, less taxes, to Britain to aid the war effort. The money came from tours and personal appearances; Cary Grant donated his salary, £31,000, from *The Philadelphia Story* to British War Relief, and Charles Laughton handed over his entire radio earnings, estimated at £1,000 a broadcast. Noel Coward's play, *Tonight at 8.30*, produced in New York raised £25,000 for the British cause.

Vivien Leigh and Laurence Olivier, starring in the Broadway production of *Romeo and Juliet* then at the 51st Theatre, said they intended to sail for home to make themselves available for military service. The play, condemned by one critic as 'a total disaster' had toured San Francisco and Chicago; also in the cast were Dame May Whitty, Alexander Knox and Cornel Wilde.

Both Olivier and Vivien Leigh had turned down all further offers from Hollywood, said to be worth over £100,000, and Miss Leigh arrived back with an Oscar as a souvenir, awarded for her performance in *Gone With the Wind*.

In London, Anthony Eden told the House of Commons that Naafi had taken £78,000 in admission charges for ENSA entertainments up to August and the artistes had been paid a total of £150,000.

This was in reply to the Conservative member for Leicester, A. M. Lyons KC, who wanted to know what capital sum had been appropriated and from what sources to maintain ENSA; what prices were charged members of the forces for admission; what proportion of persons employed in connection with the establishment were salaried; and what was the aggregate monthly amount paid in salaries, wages and fees respectively? He was also curious to learn whether and when and by whom any audit of the accounts were made and published.

Eden explained that ENSA had no funds and that there was no capital involved. Charges for admission were 3d and 6d for other ranks and NCOs, and one shilling for officers; no members of ENSA were salaried as such and payment might be made to artistes only for the entertainment in which they took part. A small staff of Naafi employees carried out administration arrangements, and as ENSA had no money of its own, the question of auditing its accounts didn't arise. The accounts of Naafi were of course subject to audit in common with the accounts of other branches of its activities.

Hannen Swaffer was more interested in the future of the Duke of Bedford and he asked whether he intended as part of his 'Peace with Hitler' proposal to hand over his estates in Devon, Cornwall, Bedfordshire, Cambridgeshire and Northamptonshire as well as the wealth from property in central London which was farmland when his ancestors acquired it.

'My remedy', Swaffer said, 'would be land nationalisation, his is social credit. Would he keep on his father's box at Drury Lane? It had its own private door, its own flunkey and its own coat of arms on the front, a fact that surprised King George VIth when he noticed it during an ENSA rehearsal. It had been the Duke's in perpetuity and when the theatre was rebuilt it cost the late Duke £300 a year. When the war came he tried to get this sum reduced; seeing ENSA shows wasn't worth so much money.'

The Daily Worker (later rechristened *The Morning Star*) turned its attention towards the end of August to the army and pointed out that, according to *The Times*, the soldiers would be attacked by the enemy of boredom during the coming winter:

It therefore wants more welfare work in addition to the entertainment provided by ENSA. Much of this so-called welfare work is really a disguised form of political work in the course of which officers, county families and local bigwigs mix up bunfights, dances, singsongs and personal advice with large doses of unadulterated Tory propaganda. Even so, welfare work has its place and the men know how to utilise it to meet their needs ... but *The Times* is sadly at fault if it imagines the only worry is that of boredom.

Judging by the letters pouring into *The Daily Worker*, their chief concern is rates of pay, food and democratic rights ...

With the Battle of Britain only days away, the War Office issued instructions through the Army Council on

7 August that 'all entertainments must be cut by fifty per cent to enable men in uniform to concentrate on the war effort and to spend as little as possible on entertainment or in bars'.

The order was issued at a time when every precaution had to be taken against the threat of imminent invasion, and it meant that the ration of entertainment per man was reduced from one show every two weeks to only one every six or nine weeks.

The effect of the order was to bring out the divisional concert party, and ENSA was able to help the khaki-clad performers by providing songs, scripts of shows and professional producers to help get the shows up on their feet.

ENSA's most successful show at the time was Archie de Bear's revue *Girls in Uniform*, an all-girl presentation with a male pianist and stage-manager.

In the USA, President Roosevelt called on his people to transform the country into an army of democracy; young men marched off for training under the first peacetime draft in the history of America, and women prepared relief parcels (known as 'Bundles for Britain') and made bandages for the Red Cross.

Armament factories produced fighting equipment for the British under the terms of the 'Lease-Lend' agreement, originally a loan of fifty destroyers in exchange for the use of strategic bases in the West Indies and later extended to the provision of arms and supplies to countries fighting the Axis powers.

'We must be', declared the President, 'the great arsenal of democracy.'

Towards the end of the first summer of the war, the Japanese invaded the French possession Dong Dang, a tiny place in Indochina, on the Chinese border. The French government sent an urgent request to America for assistance, and Roosevelt allegedly replied that 'The United States does not intend to go to war for any Ding Dong.'

For 129 years in peace and war the Royal Philharmonic
Society have given their concert in London every winter and
they see no reason why Hitler should stop them. The
concert will go on at Queen's Hall on Saturday afternoon
with Malcolm Sargent conducting.

News Item, November 1940

One night in 1940 a provincial theatre was showered with
incendiary bombs and then set rocking by high explosives.
A retired stage electrician remembers:

'It was a bit thick while it lasted. It's a queer thing how
one or two people always lose their nerve in a theatre if the
lights suddenly go. There doesn't have to be a war on. And
that's what happened then.

'About threequarters full we were and though the guns
were banging away outside the audience seemed happy
enough. Of course they didn't know the roof was burning.

'Then all the lights failed and some of the company produced torches and tried to keep everyone amused while I
groped around looking for the fault. I was afraid it might
have been general and then we couldn't have done a damn
thing.

'By this time one or two women were becoming hysterical
and as there was no time to carry out ordinary repairs I
grabbed a strip of eight bulbs on a long flex and connected

it to a small generator. Then six of the actors held the flex and stood downstage, shining the lights on the audience and making jokes about catching them at it in the back stalls.

'We managed to get them all into a shelter before firemen rushed into the building to say the roof was unsafe. Some of us stayed to give them a hand but we couldn't do much to prevent the damage. It burned for hours and all that was left next morning was a blackened shell.'

Actors in Shakespeare's time were frequently forced to leave London to go on tour, and during the reign of King James some of them travelled as far north as Aberdeen.

Those early tours were not the result of people in Cleethorpes or Carlisle clamouring for entertainment; they depended on the state of health of the capital. In a London whose water supply was maintained by water carriers with muddy jars on their backs (the citizens were afraid to wash in it, let alone drink it), and whose street cleaning was left to birds of prey, plagues were a constant hazard. As the mortality rate rose, theatres, as likely centres of infection, were shut down and the actors, deprived of a living, were forced to become strolling players once again.

The more things change, as the French proverb says, the more they stay the same, and a similar thing happened in London in wartime. When the blitz started in September 1940 the city ceased to be the centre of the theatre and actors had to take to the road.

With the dispersal of parts of the population as air-raids increased, a number of smaller provincial theatres, regarded in peacetime as 'number three' dates, became major league for West-End managements able to offer top attractions and the pick of the pack in star names. The north-west was particularly favoured, with Blackpool the base for show business during the winter of 1940–1 and a number of new productions opening there instead of London.

The Victoria Theatre in Burnley, previously a town noted only for its cotton, weaving and coal, became a haven for the bombed-out Old Vic and Sadler's Wells companies—then the nearest thing to a national theatre—and the local inhabitants were able to enjoy a season of Sybil Thorndike in Shakespeare, the heady melodies of opera that was very grand indeed, and prestige ballet presented with elegant zest. In fact, they talked of little else in Burnley for some time to come.

Tours of the classics organised by CEMA went out from Burnley to other industrial towns and mining villages in Lancashire, Durham and South Wales. Travelling light and with a minimum of props and costumes, the companies presented *Macbeth*, *The Merchant of Venice* and *Candida* to audiences in miners' halls and schools.

Dame Sybil Thorndike remembered opening in Newport in the middle of an air-raid and touring South Wales 'with a wonderful company that included our daughter Ann Casson, and Freda Gaye.

'We tried out *Candida* on them but they didn't like it so it was eventually dropped. Despite the air-raids, no one ever left the audience and we just carried on with the play; invariably in Wales, at the end of the show they all sang hymns and we couldn't stop them. They'd sing us three or four different ones and of course we had to move on to the next town. They were still singing as we waved goodbye from the coach.

'We used to love staying in the miners' homes; the houses were all so clean and they always had such very good coal fires. One village was full of children evacuated from London and when we arrived I heard one ask, "which one's the dame?" Another little girl laughed and said, "Don't be stupid. They're all dames."

'And then at Tenby we had an afternoon get-together with some of the more prominent townspeople, and I was introduced to them by an elderly clergyman who said, "I'm delighted to have the pleasure of welcoming Dame Sybil Thorndike to our town, a famous member of the oldest profession in the world."

'I didn't have the heart to tell him I understood it was the second oldest. That night a miner came backstage after watching *Medea* to say: "This is the play for us. It kindles the fires, you see."

'I was delighted because I've always felt that's what actors should try to do, kindle fires. It's funny but when ENSA heard we were touring plays like *Macbeth* and *Medea* they all said, "Oh God help the poor miners!" But Lewis [her husband, Lewis Casson] told them he knew what the miners wanted, "I know my own people and they always prefer tragedy to comedy."

'And he was absolutely right. They did.'

Freda Gaye remembers playing Portmadoc (the home of the Cassons) before going to Burnley to join another company with Sonia Dresdel, Renee Asherson and Ernest Milton.

'We toured the north before going back to London to play matinées of *Medea* at the New Theatre, and after that it was back to Wales again with the same play. It was because some people thought Greek tragedy would be too much for the miners that *Candida* was added to the repertoire, but as it turned out they all loved *Medea* and didn't like *Candida*. We were fortunate with *Medea* because Paul Schofield joined the cast. As one Welshman in the audience said, "There was no light pastry in the play. It was all solid meat."'

The Old Vic stayed closed until 1950 when it became the 'temporary' home of the National Theatre, and Sadler's Wells was converted into a rest home for people in the locality who were bombed out and remained as such until it too was damaged in 1941.

The ballet company made the New Theatre their wartime headquarters when not on tour, but there were fewer young male dancers in the new productions of Ashton's *The Wanderer* and de Valois' *Orpheus and Eurydice*. Like many actors, they had been called for military service.

Between 7 September and 2 November 1940 London was bombed on fifty-seven consecutive nights, and the air-raids went on throughout the winter. The authorities believed the raids were a foretaste of an attempted German invasion which would probably be made as soon as conditions were favourable. Orders were issued for the Home Guard to stand by, but unfortunately local commanders became confused and some of them ordered church bells to be rung in the belief the invasion had started. (The intention had been that the bells should be rung only as a warning that enemy paratroopers were landing.)

Not particularly impressed with field or woodland or the smell of earth, Michael Caine got back to the Elephant and Castle in time for the blitz:

'I used to lie in bed listening to the explosions of the bombs dropping all around the river, and as the anti-aircraft guns went off I kept hearing an odd kind of a "ping" sound. At first I had no idea where it was coming from and then it occurred to me it must have been the echo of the guns vibrating the bedsprings. It was fine when you got used to it.

'When things got really bad I was sent away again, but this time to a farm in Norfolk and I stayed there until the war ended. I had a great time helping on the farm.

'One thing I remember we used to do there. If an aircraft crashed near us we'd try to get there before the police to take the perspex off the windscreens and we'd carve rings out of it for our girl friends.

'Later on I realised, from being parted from my family at such an early age, that children should be left with their parents as much as they can while they're young. It's made me very much against the idea of boarding-schools today.'

To four-year-old Tommy Steele the bombing of the Old Kent Road meant 'that every night was Guy Fawkes night'. He remembers the sound of the sirens and the roar of the anti-aircraft guns and the night he was dragged down to the shelter on the docks wearing only a short little vest. It wasn't the fear of the bombs or the noise of the explosions that worried him; it was the possibility of all the people in the shelter seeing his little naked bottom that made him ashamed.

His mother didn't allow him to be evacuated. As far as she was concerned it would have been just like the old hop-picking days, he'd only have come back covered in fleas. So Tommy stayed put in the Old Kent Road and even got used to 'waking up covered in broken glass every morning'.

Elsie Randolph was living in Baker Street at Chalfont Court: 'People told me I should bring my mother back from the south coast because of the invasion threat.

'Although I felt she was really too ill to be moved, I rang up Jack Bentley the Rolls Royce dealer and asked if he had a decent car to spare. He immediately sent round a large Daimler and we were able to put a stretcher inside for mother.

'The same night I installed her in my top-floor flat, a landmine was dropped just next to Madame Tussaud's along the street. I couldn't begin to tell you what it was like that night with bombs falling all over the place and shop windows splintering the length of Baker Street. All you could hear was screaming and cries for help; people being dragged out of bed and bodies dragged out of the ruins, it went on all the next day.

'The water mains were hit and they had to open a pipe in the middle of the road. I was out there, bundled up in an odd assortment of clothes, hair all over the place, looking absolutely ghastly, trying to get some water, and I bumped into the actor Bill Mollison who was living at Chiltern Court. I was terribly embarrassed because he'd only ever seen me in my glamorous actress outfit before. I said: "Isn't it awful, Bill, I've got no water?"

' "It's bloody disastrous," he replied, "I've got no flat!" '

The bombings weren't confined to London; Merseyside, Tyneside, Bristol, Plymouth, Birmingham and the industrial Midlands had their share of destruction. On 15 November the concentrated attack was launched on Coventry, not only on industrial plants but also the residential area, which led to the neologism coined by the Nazis, '*Coventrysieren*': to destroy a town the way Coventry was destroyed.

A London actress working in the theatre at Coventry remembers when the raids started and 'as the few people who came to the show were asked to stay at the back of the pit we played to an apparently empty theatre.

'The *Luftwaffe* staged a dress-rehearsal of their own for the big raid on the night of the full moon, and we had to leave the stage door and make for the shelter of a pub across the road. We stayed there for a time and eventually felt we really had to get back to the digs to learn our lines for the next week's play, so we dashed out and then an air-raid warden shouted at us to take shelter. We ran down the stairs into the basement of the big store, Owen Owens, and crowded on to a bench. There was a terrible "crump" sound and then silence.

'Someone screamed out that the warden had been hit and that water was flooding down, so we all scrambled up the stairs, tripping over broken wax models and cutting ourselves on broken glass; God knows how we finally made it back to the digs.

'When the landlady came in to call me the next morning the first thing she said was, "Your theatre's gone. I'm told it's had a direct hit."

'I went along to see for myself. The worst part was the smell of charred wood and the rubble lying around everywhere. The theatre was finished but all I saw was my wardrobe floating about in five feet of water. That was the end of that and I was out of work once again.'

It was the night when Coventry-born Billie Whitelaw, then six years of age, saw her home destroyed by an enemy bomb. Her family were forced to move to Bradford, and a few years later she began her career as a child actress at the Bradford Civic Playhouse before broadcasting for the BBC's North Region at Manchester.

'From the age of eleven until I was sixteen I was in over 500 broadcasts and even played Heathcliff as a young boy in *Wuthering Heights*. It was very hard work in those days; we used to churn out two radio shows a week, live.'

Pat Kirkwood remembers the blitz as the time George Black took her out of *Black Velvet* to star in a new revue, *Top of the World*, with Flanagan and Allen and Tommy Trinder.

'We started rehearsals during the blitz and struggled on until the dress rehearsal which we did in front of a specially invited audience of soldiers. As it was impossible to tour just then we had to open cold at the Palladium on the Tuesday night and throughout the week bombs were dropping. The theatre used to shake on its foundations and one night the main swing doors blew in, covering the audience in broken glass but we still managed to put the show on and get back home unscathed. Then came a message from Charles Henry the producer that we would have to close.

'We found out afterwards that a landmine had dropped and was caught up on the roof of the Palladium. It had been hanging there all the time we'd been on stage doing the show.'

For Tommy Trinder it was the time he broke a record. 'We were in the theatre until all hours and one night George Black came round and asked me to pop along to the Hippodrome and the Holborn Empire to help things out a little, so I decided to find out how many theatres I could play in a single night. Bud Flanagan lent me his tin hat and I went off in my MG sports car. In spite of the difficulty getting about in the blackout, and even though there was an air-raid at the time, I managed to do twenty-seven theatres, one after another.'

At the height of the blitz all the London theatres were forced to close again – all, that is, except the Windmill where the 138th edition of *Revuedeville* began. Among the cast then was Eric Woodburn who later became better known on television as 'Doctor Snoddie' in the *Doctor Finlay's Casebook* series. Most of the company lived in the theatre with the girls all sleeping in the lounge, transformed into a communal dormitory. Male members of the show included three privates in the Home Guard, two auxiliary firemen and fourteen qualified ambulance men. And although high-explosive and incendiary bombs dropped all round the building, killing one of the stage staff and badly injuring dancer Joan Jay, the show still went on.

The entertainers most affected by the closure were the musicians; 300 were put out of work when the music-halls shut down; 340 when theatres shared the same fate, and 150 more when the cinemas failed to open. Night clubs had to let their 250 instrumentalists go, and the remaining 550 from hotels and dance-halls made over 3,000 on the Musicians' Union's unemployed list.

'There is no likelihood of any material improvement in the entertainment industry,' declared the union, 'but although the outlook is truly desperate, if people can't come to the music, then music must go to the people.'

A mass meeting was held to air the grievances of the musicians and to complain of 'the pitifully inadequate help given by ENSA'. It was suggested that musicians could be employed in the evenings in deep bomb-proof shelters, and mobile units could be formed to play for civil-defence workers and people using the communal feeding centres. These wartime restaurants were known to Londoners as 'Central 'Eating'.

It didn't take the buskers long to cash in on the air-raids. These accordionists, paper-tearers, strong-men and soliloquisers went into the shelters at night, vying with one another to get their acts approved, and doing good business once the hat was passed round. But with actors and instrumentalists anxious to instal platforms in the shelters for organised entertainment, many Londoners were more anxious to get a decent night's sleep.

As a result of negotiations with the Ministry of Labour, ENSA staged some special shelter shows and gave concerts at rest centres where the homeless were given refuge. CEMA produced Sunday concerts at Wigmore Hall, and also arranged for musicians to perform in shelters as solo artistes. Variety shows went into London shelters twice a week, and BBC's popular feature *In Town Tonight* was transmitted from a shelter at the beginning of November. These broadcasts were not pre-recorded, but people taking part were able to stay in the new underground studios if they were unable to get home during an air-raid.

Shelter marshals at Aldwych tube station were less than happy about the publicity given to an ENSA concert; there were so many extra customers they were forced to close the gates early. But it soon became a feature of the shelter to offer nightly entertainment from actors who had been working in nearby theatres before the shut down.

Stephen Williams, liaison officer between the BBC and ENSA, had a difficult job during the blitz. He had to provide weekly broadcasts, on Saturday evenings, of ENSA shelter shows but he also had to make sure these shows didn't attract people who were merely looking for free entertainment. He had to avoid bringing in star names in case the shelter in use became too overcrowded, and yet the artistes had to be good enough for radio. During the first broadcast from Aldwych station, singer Pat Taylor had to struggle to maintain rhythm to a sporadic accordion accompaniment; a man sang 'The Changing of the Guard' with some assistance from the shelterers, and a woman in the audience burst into the opening chorus of 'Because' without a word of warning.

Another problem was caused by overcrowding at nearby Holborn station. People unable to find a place there simply walked along the deserted tunnel to Aldwych. The track was eventually boarded up and bunks erected to hold 2,000 people.

Londoners quickly discovered how to evade the regulation that tried to prevent them from using the stations before 4 pm. The rule caused queues of women and children to line up well before the time with the hope of getting good places on platforms and along passageways.

Not even the first in the queue were allowed down until

the appointed time, and yet they still found people already there, with blankets to reserve spaces for latecomers. The queue dodgers simply went into a station as passengers, carrying small bags (concealing a blanket), and after they boarded a train they were able, with careful timing, to get back to the original station just before the regulation hour when out would come the blanket.

Margaretta Scott was at the Apollo Theatre, playing in *Margin for Error*, when the blitz began; Michael Redgrave was at the Globe next door in *Thunder Rock*, which had transferred from the tiny Neighbourhood Theatre.

'During one big raid,' she said, 'the audiences from both the Globe and the Lyric came into the Apollo and Michael joined us onstage to help with an impromptu entertainment until the raid finished at four o'clock in the morning. We sang and told stories and the audience joined us in a sing-song. At three o'clock I went to have a drink in Michael's dressing-room, and when I got back my dresser Kitty was on the stage singing an old-time music-hall song; she brought the house down. 'It's a strange thing but I can't remember ever being at all nervous during the raids.'

Constance Cummings had finished touring *The Outsiders*, a play with John Clements co-starring which had gone round garrison theatres after a brief commercial tour.

'It was a marvellously old-fashioned story, all about a crippled girl whose father was a Harley Street surgeon. All his medical friends had failed to cure her and along came this dazzling foreigner who helps her, and naturally she fell in love with him. I believe the authoress walked on at the end of the first night when it was produced in London . . . on crutches. There were memorable curtain lines in it like,

> *Father*: You're leaving me then?
> *Daughter*: I must go, Father. I want life.
> *Father* (to dazzling foreigner): So you're taking my daughter?
> *Foreigner*: No sir. I'm taking my degree.

'We were also making a film with Emlyn Williams at Elstree at the same time, staying at the local golf club. It was terribly nerve-wracking with the blitz in full spate. We'd never know if everyone would manage to turn up for work.'

Florence Desmond had been working at the Café de Paris, doing her impersonations and singing a song called 'I've Got the Deepest Shelter in Town' when she was booked by George Black for his revue *Apple Sauce*, with Max Miller, Vera Lynn and Doris Hare.

Then she learned from her doctor that she was pregnant again. She explained to George Black and Val Parnell; they said she should go ahead and have the baby and not worry about the show. Again she lost the baby when it was born prematurely in October.

Five years earlier she became very ill during the London run of *Seeing Stars* and blood tests showed she was suffering from lead poisoning, caused by using a carmine greasepaint on her mouth that was found to contain 42 per cent lead.

It was a country doctor who first hit on the reason for her sickness. He had been in Sheffield during World War I and discovered that some of his patients, women factory workers, were contracting lead poisoning and consequently miscarrying. They had found out that by scraping the ointment off belladonna plasters and swallowing it, they were able to abort unwanted babies; the lead content softened the uterus. No one realised then that the condition was irreversible and the damage permanent.

Apple Sauce opened at the Holborn Empire and closed three weeks later. On 14 October the theatre suffered a direct hit and was reduced to a heap of rubble.

Doris Hare recalls: 'We tried to keep going in spite of the blitz, but we were bombed out. When the siren sounded we'd just go on and do improvisations until the all clear went; the audience always stayed, no matter how severe the raids were.

'After the show closed I went to Bristol for the BBC and

worked all during the raids there. Very Lynn was singing in the studio at the same time and I remember the producer Howard Thomas [as a BBC producer, he began the *Brains Trust* broadcasts, and as managing director of ABC Television he was one of the pioneers of commercial television in Britain] telling us he was going to make her a big star. During a broadcast of *Ack-ack, Beer-beer*, he told me he'd like me to do a new show called *Shipmates Ashore*: "It needs a warm personality."

'It was originally intended for a six-week run, but went on for the next five and a half years. It was intended for the men in the merchant navy and we would announce the birth of babies to sailors away from home. Stuart Hibberd made the announcements and one time the Crazy Gang were guest artistes and they changed all his cue-cards around. He didn't know where he was and ended up by saying that "the Merchant Navy has given birth to twins".'

A few minutes before midnight on 15 October 1940 Drury Lane Theatre was bombed. A 500lb bomb had fallen through the roof, gallery, upper circle and grand circle to explode finally at the back of the stalls. The nose cap went through the auditorium, smashing rows of seats beneath it, but fortunately the safety curtain, which took the full force of the blast, saved the stage. Although the royal box was undamaged and the bomb narrowly missed the 'Ghost's Walk', thirty minutes later several incendiaries fell, destroying most of the orchestra stalls. Next morning the auditorium was a mess, sodden seats, shattered woodwork and chandeliers and thick plaster dust everywhere.

That same night the manager of ENSA's Variety Section, ex-acrobat Bob Ricardo was blown out of the window of his flat, which received a direct hit, and he landed on a heap of rubble in the back yard still holding the kettle he'd been putting on the stove for a cup of tea.

ENSA's work went on without interruption, preparing for the demands of the winter. Twenty-eight garrison theatres were open and smaller theatres had also been set up at 120 RAF stations. Entertainment was restored to its pre-Dunkirk output, and a 50 per cent increase in shows meant bigger productions like *Funny Face* and *1066 and All That* going into rehearsal.

Apart from concert parties touring 'with big stars' there were 'Nanki-Poo' type shows given by solo artistes at anti-aircraft and searchlight sites because the 'sing-song spirit was all-important'. The forces favourite turns were listed, in order of preference, soubrettes; accordionists; 'good' bands; songs they could all sing; 'good' ballads; and women 'dressed up in fancy costumes'. Demands for straight plays and potted versions of Shakespeare also increased, and by the end of 1940, 7 million troops had seen 40,000 shows.

There were no ENSA pantomimes that year, but Lupino Lane was cast as the first 'male' Aladdin for many years in the production at Nottingham with Pat Kirkwood; Stanley Holloway, Patricia Burke and Leslie Henson were in *Robinson Crusoe* at the Palace, Manchester, and Tommy Trinder was in the same city, starring in *Cinderella* at the Opera House; Jack Buchanan was at the Royal Theatre in Birmingham, and the hit songs from the Christmas shows included 'When Our Dreams Grow Old', 'With a Smile on Our Lips' and 'Behind the Clouds'.

The big circuses had closed down and the clowns, acrobats and animal acts were scattered all over the world. There was no Bertram Mills circus at Olympia and no circus at the Agricultural Hall, Islington, although Manchester and Edinburgh managed to have their normal winter seasons. And while a few had gone into ENSA, hundreds of circus artistes, trainers, carpenters and electricians were out of work.

Coco the clown, the Russian who became top funny man in British circus rings, the man who fought for Imperial Russia in World War I and for the Latvian army during the revolution, became at forty-one Private Nicholai Poliakoff in the British army in 1940.

He was invalided out a year later and joined ENSA, staying with the organisation until 1945. After the war he went back to the now-disbanded Bertram Mills circus to spend forty-eight years with them altogether. He joined Roberts Brothers circus some time before he died on 26 September 1974.

The Windmill gave a Christmas show for the RAF, with Valerie Tandy and Charmian Innes, both of them qualified in first-aid to help during the blitz. The only West-End pantomime was at the Coliseum. Vic Oliver replaced John Gielgud in the tour of Coward's *Red Peppers* and Alastair Sim, touring in a new play, *Cottage to Let*, opened at the Theatre Royal, Glasgow, with Leslie Banks, Gillian Lind and young George Cole in the cast.

George Cole made his first appearance as a boy actor in *White Horse Inn* at the Grand Theatre, Blackpool, in 1939; he made his West-End début when *Cottage to Let* opened at Wyndham's in 1941.

Two other successful tours were *Women Aren't Angels* with Robertson Hare, Alfred Drayton and Gordon Harker; and *On Approval* with Diana Churchill, her husband Barry K. Barnes, Cathleen Nesbitt and Roland Culver.

Wyndhams Theatre opened for afternoon performances with singer Irene Eisinger and Edith Evans reading poetry. Dame Edith, who started her working life as an apprentice milliner in Buckingham Palace Road, once said that as a girl she had to earn her living somehow and there was no question of going on the stage. 'That happened by chance when a producer met me and asked me to act. I've always been asked, you know. I never offer myself.'

Leonard Sachs, who recreated the beery free-and-easy atmosphere of the Victorian music-hall in Covent Garden, was bombed out but he found new premises to reopen his old-time show in Albemarle Street, just behind the old Berkeley Hotel.

British soldiers based in Iceland saw their first ENSA shows and complained about the beer in the Naafi canteens: 'It was so weak it could barely stand upright in the bottle' and the only other drink available was a local brew called 'Black

Death', as lethal as Red Biddy.

On 19 December a Mr Muff, the Socialist Member of Parliament for Kingston-upon-Hull, complained to the War Minister about a report from an officer commanding a coastal battery 'expressing disapproval of the officers and men of a vulgar entertainment given on 2 December'; what steps did he propose to take in view of the increasing number of such entertainments provided by ENSA?

The War Office (in a written reply) said: 'The complaint has been brought to our notice and immediate steps have been taken to have the offending act withdrawn.'

Dr Edith Summerskill, then the Labour Member of Parliament for West Fulham, asked the government to deal with sanitation in Underground stations and shelters immediately as 'within a mile of the House there existed conditions that would have made a member of a primitive African tribe shudder', and she had seen many nasty cases of people suffering from 'shelter legs', swollen legs due to lack of proper sleep.

'If ENSA could go to the shelters,' she said, 'then why not doctors?' People would surely enjoy their visits as much if not more than an ENSA concert because, in her experience, there was nothing people liked better than hearing their bodies discussed in detail – as long as it was in simple language. Another nasty complaint was 'shelter throat', caused by breathing dust in the cheaply built shelters.

'The best play of the year', according to the critics, was Emlyn Williams's *The Light of Heart*, with Angela Baddeley, Godfrey Tearle and Gladys Henson.

In his curtain speech, Tearle told the audience that the author had been in the Home Guard at the time when five million British stood together facing the enemy, but 'he is valuable to the theatre. Cherish him'.

Emlyn Williams's earlier success, *The Corn is Green*, had been produced on Tuesday, 26 November at the National Theatre, West 41st Street, New York with Ethel Barrymore in the lead.

It also had opened to highly critical approval and was the season's first legitimate hit. 'What a fine actress Miss Barrymore is,' wrote Walter Winchell, 'the first lady, indeed. See her newest hit and be exhilarated.'

'This is in gratitude for *The Corn Is Green*,' wrote critic Alexander Woolcott to the play's producer, Herman Shumlin. 'That nourishing play at the National renews my faith in the eternal theatre. All the days of your life you will be glad you produced it and gave it your best. Words fail me, and it serves me right for having squandered them on lesser occasions, when I try to tell people of the glory that is Ethel Barrymore. As I go about my daily chores the memory of her mettlesome and gallant performance lingers like a glow at the hearth. Of course the final scene is the more moving because somehow it tops the reservoir of unshed tears which must be full to the brim in these grievous days; in that scene Miss Barrymore is radiant with a light that is not on land or sea . . .'

The day *The Corn Is Green* opened on Broadway was the day Elaine Barry, the fourth Mrs John Barrymore, was granted a divorce in Hollywood from the actor 'with capricious tendencies for self-ruination who had been acclaimed as the first Hamlet of his generation'. He had less than two years left to live.

It was around this time that Lana Turner, typical MGM product and studio property, eloped with band-leader Artie Shaw, the first of her many husbands; they married in Las Vegas. She told the Press later that such an elopement was typical of Hollywood in those days.

Gertrude Lawrence consented to take charge of ENSA broadcasts to be recorded in New York. The first recording took place on Friday, 13 December and featured Hildegarde, Ella Shields, Harry Richman and a Major Bowes, the first man to popularise amateur discoveries on radio.

He had also been given the credit some five years earlier for finding an unknown twenty-year-old singer and teaming him with a trio to rename it 'The Hoboken Four', giving

Frank Sinatra his first break in show business.

At twenty, Sinatra, already gifted with a magnetic personality, 'possessed a satiny voice that made most girls sigh'. His work with Major Bowes led to the next booking, and he became resident singer at the Rustic Cabin, a night-club located on Route 9W, near Englewood, New Jersey.

It has been suggested that a dubious character named Willie Moretti fixed Sinatra's first singing job at the Rustic Cabin for $35 a week, but Sinatra said years later that this was untrue: 'I never even heard of Willie Moretti until 1944. A friend of mine, a musician, introduced me to Harold Arlen who had the band at the club. He gave me a start at $15 a week and I stayed with him for the next eighteen months. No mob got me my first break.'

> It's not true that Hitler dropped Hess on Scotland because
> he was short of bombs.
>
> *ENSA Comedian*, 1941

In 1941 the Germans invaded Russia; the British army
marched into Benghazi, and the Royal Navy sank the
battleship *Bismarck*; the aircraft-carrier *Ark Royal* was
torpedoed in the Mediterranean, and the Japanese attacked
Pearl Harbour. It was the year Britain and the USA declared
war on Japan.

On the morning of 5 January that year Amy Johnson
took off from Blackpool airport on a routine ferrying flight
to Kidlington, near Oxford. In the afternoon her aircraft,
100 miles off course, crashed into the Thames estuary not far
from a naval convoy. No one will ever know what happened
before the crash; her body was never found.

James Joyce, whose book *Ulysses* profoundly influenced
the language and style of twentieth-century writing, died on
13 January in Zürich, aged fifty-nine.

On the evening of 10 May a Messerschmitt 110 flew over
the Scottish coast and its sole occupant, Hitler's deputy
Rudolph Hess, baled out and landed in a field. The self-
appointed ambassador had come to discuss peace terms, but
he was interned and has been in Spandau jail for over thirty
years.

The English novelist and critic Virginia Woolf died in May. When the air-raids began in 1940 she had moved from Mecklenburgh Square, Bloomsbury, down to Sussex but her nervous system, never robust, collapsed under the strain of it all and she drowned herself.

The formula for success in the commercial theatre in 1941 seemed to be displays of undernourished nudity or naughty-knickers whimsey; anything went as long as it was spicy, titillating and inadequately clothed.

According to columnist Gordon Beckles, 'The tendency of the moment is to see young ladies disporting themselves in their birthday suits. Incidentally, I wonder how many people know that the "altogether" is OK by the LCC [London County Council] so long as it does not move in public? Which explains the elaborate stage candelabra and sparkling fountains. Bare bottoms and Bach will always be good enough for me.'

It was not good enough for Charles F. Smith, a director of Brighton's Theatre Royal. A wealthy Leeds manufacturer, he had founded the Civic Arts Theatre there as well as the Bradford Civic Centre. A number of actors, including Eric Portman, got their first chance because of him. Smith had retired to Brighton some years before the war and took an active interest in the live theatre and was concerned at the poor quality, not only of commercial shows, but also of some of ENSA's offerings. He also disagreed with ENSA's policy of categorising their companies into A, B, C or D units, with the biggest A units visiting places like Aldershot and only playing in garrison theatres; leaving the more remote places to accordionists and lady sopranos touring in small vans.

He felt it was wrong for anti-aircraft sites to have inferior shows, while main service bases got the top stars and finest productions and, true to his beliefs, he personally financed Mobile Entertainments Southern Area (MESA), sending two plays and two variety companies out every night to tour Southern Command, then reaching from the Kent coast across to Hampshire. MESA travelled in single-decker buses which also carried props and scenery.

Included in the cast of an early MESA play, *George and Margaret*, was a young student from Ditchling, in Sussex, who had originally planned to become an architect. Through the fortunes of war Donald Sinden went into the theatre.

'Until 1940 I had no interest in the stage whatsoever, although my sister Joy and brother Leon [who also turned professional] were keen amateurs, always rehearsing something or other along with cousin Frank at the Brighton Little Theatre.

'Frank and I got our call-up papers at the same time and the RAF wanted him there and then. Naturally he was in the middle of rehearsals for a new play so he asked me to take over his part.

'"Don't be bloody silly, Frank," I said, "I've never done anything like that before." But of course I couldn't let him down and as soon as I'd got the greasepaint on I was hooked.'

Charles Smith saw the show and invited Donald to join MESA. This was at the beginning of 1941 when he had been turned down by the navy because of asthma and he was told to do some kind of war work. Smith put in an application on his behalf and as MESA qualified by this time as grade-two war work, he was given permission to join the company.

Donald Sinden made his first professional appearance for 7s 6d a performance, in front of a service audience, in *George and Margaret* on 26 January 1941.

Sinden continues: 'Lots of service people were keen to join us when they were on leave... We played mainly in Nissen huts and village halls, anywhere we could put up a stage, and the men in the company were responsible for the scenery and the girls looked after the props and furniture. We averaged six shows a week and every night we packed the whole thing up and drove back to Brighton.

'Some of the places were incredibly small and one stage was so minute we had to use two card-tables to represent a sideboard and a dining-table. We had to carry our chairs on and off as we made our various entrances and exits and because of the shortage of fruit, the bowl on the sideboard contained a battered wax banana and some tennis-balls painted to look like apples. The stage had been assembled from table tops and when a rather heavily built actor jumped up from his chair it split down the middle and all the fruit bounced over the footlights on to the floor. There never was a better cue for someone to ask: "Tennis, anyone?"'

According to theatre critics, another promising newcomer was Barbara Mullen who, having taken over Celia Johnson's part in *Rebecca* some months earlier, was back in the West End in *Jeannie*.

'*Jeannie* was very much of a surprise for me,' she said, 'and one of the nicest experiences was working in *Rebecca* with Owen Nares and Margaret Rutherford. She was a delight to work with and lovely in the most literal sense of the word.'

She starred with Eric Portman and Albert Lieven in *Jeannie*, and was also cast in the film of the play with Kay Hammond and Michael Redgrave, staying in London for most of the war in a flat somewhere between Buckingham Palace and Victoria station.

'It became known as a lucky flat, although it seemed to be all glass with a huge skylight. But it was never hit and all kinds of people would come and stay the night, sometimes as many as forty and I don't know to this day who most of them were. We never had enough mattresses to go round, but they'd sleep on the floor while all around us houses were falling to the ground and people were being killed.

'There was one terrible night when a bomb dropped on Wellington Barracks and 158 bodies were brought out from the ruined building, and another night I was playing darts in a pub with my husband, and some houses up the street got a direct hit. There we were singing songs at the top of our voices while they were taking the dead out of a house a hundred yards away.

'Later on I visited RAF stations with a variety show and I also recorded "Danny Boy"; I believe it still sells today. And I had to travel to Bangor for BBC broadcasts, standing

Jack Buchanan and Elsie Randolph. They went to France in 1940 with one of the first companies to entertain the soldiers of the British Expeditionary Forces stationed along the Maginot Line.

Above left: Terry-Thomas. He enjoyed modest success in cabaret until World War II when he joined ENSA. He was later called up into the army to become a 'Star in Battledress'.

Above right: Dick Emery. He was born into the business but didn't try comedy until he became a member of one of Ralph Reader's RAF Gang Shows.

Left: Arthur Lowe. If it hadn't been for the War and the need to entertain his fellow soldiers stationed on the Gaza Strip he might never have become a professional actor.

Deborah Kerr. Discovered by agent
John Gliddon while working at the
Open-Air Theatre, Regent's Park, she
went into films to be named as 'the first
blackout film star'.

Right: Patrick Cargill. He worked in a repertory theatre at Bexhill until he rejoined the army and was posted to India where he became an entertainments officer. (*Thames Television*)

Below: Henry Oscar. Seen here in his Drury Lane office, Henry Oscar was ENSA's drama director.

Basil Dean. As a result of his experience putting on troops shows in World War I he was able to set up ENSA almost as soon as World War II began.

Above left: Pat Kirkwood. She had great success in *Black Velvet* early on in the War and soon became known in London as 'Britain's first wartime stage star'.

Above right: Donald Sinden. Unable to join the services for health reasons he went into an entertainment unit that toured the south coast before crossing over to France after D-Day. He finished the War entertaining the troops in the Far East.

Left: Dame Sybil Thorndike. She helped Dame Lilian Braithwaite form the Military Hospitals Section of ENSA before taking out a company with her husband Lewis Casson to entertain the miners of South Wales.

Right: Ralph Reader. 'King of the RAF *Gang Shows*.'

The Theatre Royal, Drury Lane. It was the official headquarters of ENSA throughout the War and most shows rehearsed on its vast stage before they were passed as suitable for forces entertainment.

Constance Cummings. With Judith Furse, she formed a company of theatrical stars that played to packed houses wherever they put on a show. (*Stuart Robinson*)

Dick Bentley broadcasting with Margaret Lockwood. He went back to Australia during the War to take a party of entertainers through the jungles of New Guinea.

Faith Brook (seated on the sofa). She appeared in the 'Stars in Battledress' production of *Flare Path* with Wilfrid Hyde White (seated at the table) and Kenneth Connor (in the doorway).

Above: Tommy Trinder. Entertaining the troops in Italy, 1944.

Right: Monty Berman. Posted to Blackpool in the RAF, he staged variety shows in the Opera House there before he was commissioned and posted to an operational station.

Bottom right: Jack Hawkins. He was posted to India and eventually became responsible – as Colonel-in-Charge of ENSA – for all troop entertainments in India and the Far East. (*Gilbert Pressenda, Nice*)

Far right: Florence Desmond. She divided her time during World War II between starring in the West End and entertaining the troops at home and overseas. (*Fox Photos*)

Previous pages: With ENSA in Gibraltar. From left to right: Michael Wilding, Jeanne de Casalis, Beatrice Lillie, John Gielgud, Phyllis Stanley, Dame Edith Evans, and Elisabeth Welch.

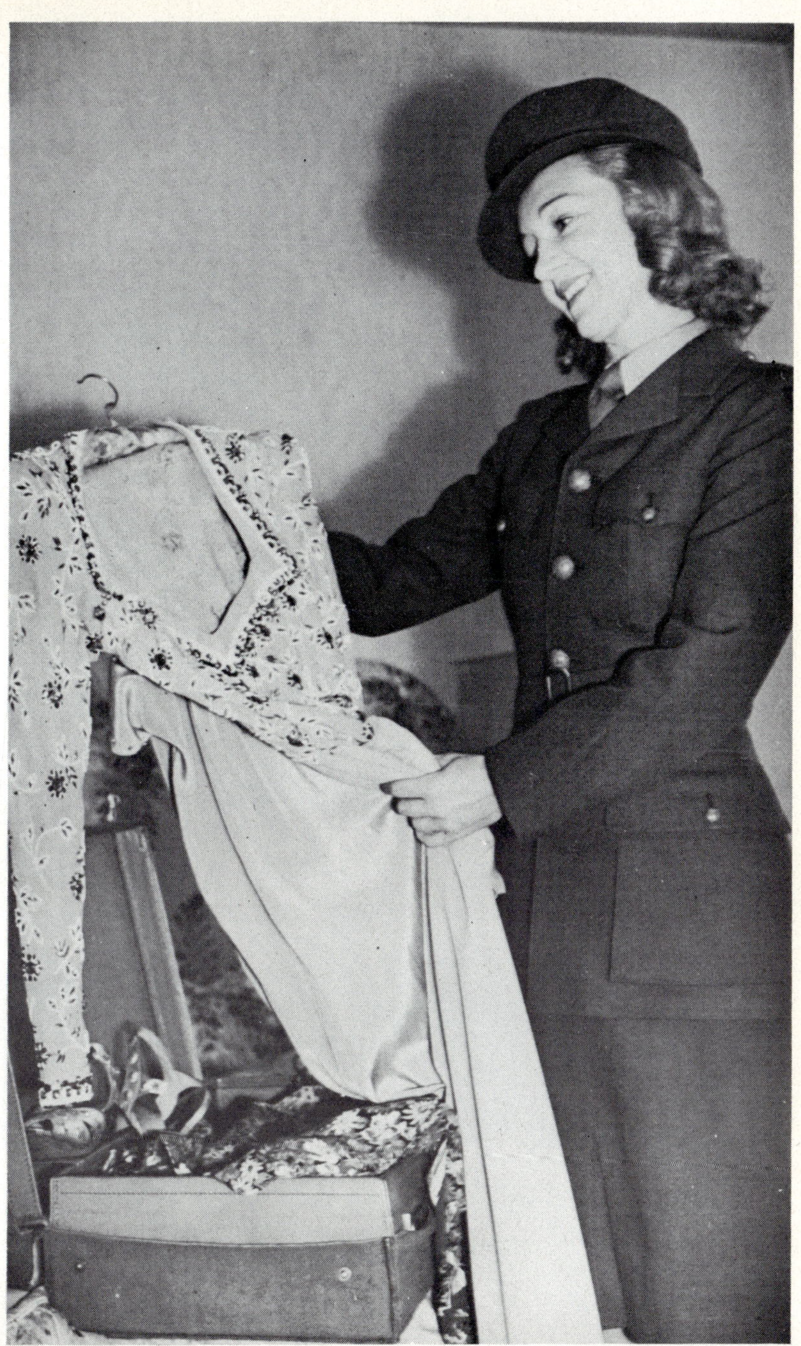

Richard Hearne. 'Mr Pastry' was in
Europe soon after D-Day and played in
towns he had first visited with his acrobat
father before the War. (*Kent Messenger*)

in the train the whole way there and possibly the sheer luxury of being able to sit on a suitcase in the corridor on the way home.

'Another poignant memory was being in the Café de Paris with Florence Desmond just two weeks before it was destroyed by a bomb.'

In the spring George Black decided to revive his revue *Apple Sauce* at the Palladium. Florence Desmond, recovered from her illness, was able to join Max Miller and Vera Lynn in a cast that included a young understudy, Jean Carr, who changed her name when she later went into films and became well known in the post-war years as Jean Kent.

Florence Desmond was also asked by the owner of the Café de Paris, a Mr Poulsen, to do a cabaret there.

'I was very busy with the revue which, despite air-raids, was doing excellent business so I turned down his offer. Two weeks later the Rialto Cinema, which was over the Café de Paris, got a direct hit and the bomb went right through the floor, killing many people in the restaurant, among them Mr Poulsen and the band-leader, Ken "Snake Hips" Johnson.'

ENSA held an Open Day at the Theatre Royal towards the end of March, and the curious were taken on a guided tour which started in the control room. They were shown the complicated card-system with company movements allocated nine weeks ahead: straight plays on green cards, orchestras on yellow, and revues suitably blue. The bare room, walls painted a dingy yellow, was once a dressing-room for Garrick as well as every male star for over 270 years.

Next door, the Green Room, where distinguished actors formerly met and talked with acquaintances, had become a cubby-hole for ENSA chorus-girls, and on the wall still hung a gilt-framed mirror in which Garrick would take a last look before he went onstage.

The splendid salon was now labelled 'Publicity Office', and occupied by W. Macqueen Pope, public-relations man and theatre historian, whose family had been connected with the Theatre Royal since 1740.

The visitors were shown the front of the house where the great auditorium had been half curtained-off to hide the effects of bomb damage and they watched a young girl, one of hundreds attending auditions, singing to stalls covered in dust sheets and to an empty royal box in which every king since Charles II had sat. From that box George II flourished the Duke of Cumberland's despatches with the news of the defeat of the Young Pretender at Culloden Moor; in 1941 the Royal Room behind the box was the factory-entertainments department.

Contracts were drawn up in the converted box office, and the famous Rotunda, where George III had publicly slapped his son, later King George IV, served as a rehearsal room for concert parties. The long Regency Bar, partitioned off into rows of hardboard-clad offices, had been nicknamed 'the last mile', and the Stalls Bar was transformed into a recording studio for ENSA broadcasts.

The staff bar was an air-raid shelter and a fifty-year-old tradition that there should always be some live goldfish in the bar was broken. They had first been used in one of Sir Augustus Harris's productions, the largest was usually named 'Gussie' in his honour, but after the bomb fell they were moved for safety to the home of a Drury Lane employee.

Down in the dungeon-like rooms beside giant columns supporting the stage, the Press men watched photographer Edgar Wrather posing ENSA artistes for passport photographs. He had been taking pictures of theatre people for nearly fifty years, and some of the thousands he photographed during the war were of actors he hadn't seen for thirty years; they had all come out of retirement to help entertain the troops.

Finally they talked to an ENSA company, *The Ten of Us*, back from Gibraltar, who told them they'd given concerts on submarines and on the deck of the *Ark Royal*: a hydraulic lift doubled as a stage and the company began their opening number in the bowels of the ship, finishing the chorus as the lift slowly rose to come to a standstill at deck level in front of the 1,200 seamen on board.

A government white paper issued in March said that 'the ENSA organisation under the general support of Naafi should henceforth be recognised as the sole supply of professional entertainments for any section of the community for whom such entertainments, other than concerts promoted by CEMA, were provided out of public or semi-public funds'.

Geraldo was appointed director of ENSA's Music Division and an advisory council was formed 'to give advice and help in any schemes which further the love of music in the services'.

Sir Henry Wood, Arnold Bax, William Walton and Sir Malcolm Sargent (who became renowned for his Promenade Concerts from 1950 until his death in 1967) served on the committee.

One aspect of musical life during the war was the remarkable rise in popularity of symphonic music when it was made accessible to audiences of servicemen and factory workers who until then had shown little signs of appreciating classical music, no doubt from lack of opportunity.

When the London Philharmonic Orchestra, conducted by Sir Malcolm Sargent, made musical history by going on tour in 1940, they were received with such enthusiasm in the Midlands and North that every hall they played was packed to overflowing, night after night.

'Symphonic music', commented critic Rollo Myers in 1945, 'was henceforth appreciated by workers and ceased from then on to be the prerogative of a musical élite.'

It was at the end of March 1941 that the War Office decided ENSA wasn't able to keep up with the demand for services entertainment. In future army shows would be presented whenever possible by the army itself. An entertainments officer was appointed for each unit to organise and maintain a concert party and a dance band with funds supplied by

Army Welfare.

A former musical director from the Coliseum Theatre, who had been ENSA's area organiser at Aldershot before going into the army, had already been presenting a forces show called *Stars in Battledress*; this was taken over and subsequently run by the army. For Basil Dean this military boot firmly wedged in the door of his hitherto civilian organisation signalled the end of ENSA's entertainment monopoly and the beginning of a series of clashes with Army Welfare.

Meanwhile the war went on and the blitz continued to disrupt theatres.

At the Saville, Leslie Henson's first revue *Up and Doing*, with Binnie Hale and Stanley Holloway, was interrupted when, within the space of a week, four bombs fell close to the theatre. But the building was patched up and the show went on and ran until March 1942.

The London Casino and the Duke of York's Theatre were damaged, and the bomb that fell on Sloane Square Underground station shut down the Royal Court.

Chelsea's only surviving theatre remained derelict until the mid-1950s, when the English Stage Company took it over. They were to gain fame with John Osborne's *Look Back in Anger* and the work of other new playwrights like Arnold Wesker and John Arden.

Elisabeth Welch, living in a mews flat off Sloane Street in 1941, was in S. N. Behrman's *No Time for Comedy* which opened in March at the Haymarket. The play had toured garrison theatres for ENSA before opening in the West End with Diana Wynyard, Lilli Palmer and Rex Harrison in the leading roles; it ran until Rex Harrison went into the RAF Volunteer Reserve in 1942.

London had been Elisabeth Welch's home since the early thirties and in spite of the bombing she didn't want to go back to New York: 'All my friends were here and I was determined to stay. It's strange when one looks back now how everyone kept on working; as soon as the siren went the show stopped for a moment and someone would say: "Will those who have to leave, or wish to leave, please do so." And then we'd take up where we left off. I still have my incendiary bomb shovel; I kept it as a souvenir.'

Apart from war news, the papers in April gave a great deal of publicity to the question of Sunday opening of theatres. For Edith Evans, then living in a flat in The Albany, Piccadilly, 'Sunday opening was the only thing I had ever sat on the fence about. My personal prejudice was to have my Sunday free. On the other hand, I enjoyed Sunday newspapers; I went to restaurants and rode on trains. If the public wanted to be entertained on Sunday, I should play with a good grace. All the same I thought it a mistake to assume beforehand that Sunday shows would be a success. They had to be proved a good thing or a bad thing. In the meantime I remained on the fence.'

But the government decided against it although actress Barbara Nixon blamed 'an unholy alliance of bishops and brewers' for the decision, and Athene Seyler pointed out that under ENSA contracts, people were obliged to work on Sundays and were not able to refuse.

However, a surprising number of stars took part in a Sunday afternoon concert in the Regal Cinema, Margate; they included Lilli Palmer, Ursula Jeans, Rex Harrison, John Clements, Roger Livesey and Naunton Wayne. The show had been organised at the beginning of May by Constance Cummings, in response to a request from a naval officer stationed at Chatham.

Constance Cummings remembered: 'We called it *You've Asked For It* and apart from the tenor Derek Oldham and our pianist Nat Ayer [who wrote "If You Were the Only Girl in the World"], all the rest were straight actors. We were all wandering around at the first rehearsal saying "What shall we do for them?" when a yummy little blonde from the Palladium, Whitey Neilson, said she could do a striptease.

'Everyone shouted, "No, no. Sit down, Whitey, that's not what they want at all" and our compère, Jack Melford, decided a good strong monologue would go down well with the navy. During that first concert as he began "The Green Eye of the Little Yellow God", Whitey crept on behind him shushing the audience and slowly did her strip during his recital. Naturally the applause was terrific and Jack was delighted, until he found out about Whitey.

'After the Chatham show word got round and lots of officers wrote asking us to put on more concerts. We did one practically every Sunday for the next two years with John Clements and me as the main organisers and all the artistes volunteered their services.

'Judith [Judith Furse and Constance Cummings originated the Chatham revue] and I sat down one day and counted how many servicemen had seen the show and we realised it must have been close to one and a quarter million, and with no assistance from ENSA. It was very tiring but somehow nobody thought about being tired in those days.

'I thought it was the very least I could do and I was doing the job I liked best.'

Another person who organised service shows without the benefit of ENSA's resources was Monty Berman, managing director of Bermans and Nathans, suppliers of costumes to theatres, films and television. Apart from war service with the RAF, all his life has been spent among actors and designers; at the age of sixteen he worked with George Black, assisting him in launching the first Crazy Gang production. Although he sold 75 per cent of Berman shares to Lord Grade's ATV company in 1964, Monty (as he is known to three generations of stage and screen stars) still regards the business as very much his own show.

Turned down by an aircrew selection board because of colour-blindness, Monty was posted to Blackpool in 1941 as an ordinary airman and billeted in a former boarding-house. Good at drill he was picked for a special 'Wings for Victory' squad and promoted to acting-corporal/drill instructor. He was also asked to stage-manage some shows being presented by Wing-Commander Bruce Sievier at the Opera House, Blackpool, and later took over production himself.

Monty recalls: 'The shows had nothing to do with ENSA, we called them "Contact" shows and all of us had to carry out normal duties during the day and get together in the evenings to rehearse. The RAF personnel did the first half of a show and the second half usually consisted of "surprise" guests, professional artistes appearing in the area. Sydney Torch, then an organist, came in to run the orchestra and we also managed to put together a small dance band . . .

'One night [a message was circulated] to say the artistes due to play the second half couldn't make it because their train was held up in an air-raid. I told Sydney Torch to go on playing the organ at the interval; I knew the Crazy Gang were in Blackpool and I sent scouts out looking for them.

'They all came along to help out, Bud Flanagan and Chesney Allen, Nervo and Knox, Naughton and Gold, Eddie Gray and one or two others. I told them we only had an hour left for the second half as the stage had to be got ready for a film later that night. Bud told me I hadn't a thing to worry about but after two and a half hours I just couldn't get them off. It was probably the most hilarious show of them all and the one we all remember.'

Monty Berman left Blackpool at the end of August and was commissioned at Uxbridge before being posted to 5 Group Bomber Command at Grantham. Promoted to Squadron-Leader, he was one of the officers organising the 'Dambusters' raid.

London's last big raid was on the night of 10 May when 300 German aircraft dropped bombs starting over 2,000 fires. A bomb fell on the Houses of Parliament and one of the few city churches to escape the Great Fire of 1666, St Olave's, was also destroyed.

The original home of the Promenade Concerts, Queen's Hall in Langham Place – around whose illuminated goldfish-pool generations of Londoners had strolled during intervals –

was reduced to a pile of smoking rubble. The London Philharmonic Orchestra was due to play there the following day and when the players arrived for rehearsal they saw nothing but a burnt-out shell; a number of valuable musical instruments, left in the hall overnight, were also destroyed. Other instruments were borrowed, a new hall was found, and the concert took place as advertised. And the 'Proms' found a new home at the Albert Hall.

Backstage in 1941 the staff were ready for anything, training as fire fighters in their spare time and taking turns roof-spotting while raids were in progress. One theatre owed its survival to a stage carpenter, Bill Thomas, who smothered incendiaries on the roof while a show was in progress; he pounced on two fire bombs and got them both out, removing all traces in less than three minutes.

At the Phoenix Theatre, blown-off doors were put back on new hinges less than thirty minutes after a bomb blast ripped everything movable wide open.

Most stage staff took turns sleeping in the theatre at night, and four of them had a narrow escape when a bomb tore a hole in one of the exterior walls, cascading tons of débris on to the floor of the stage. Fortunately the stage had been reinforced shortly after war broke out and it carried the whole load; four men sleeping underneath crawled out with nothing worse than a headache as rescue workers feverishly searched for them in the wreckage.

While the Shaftesbury, Queen's and Palace Theatres may have presented a somewhat gaunt and scorched appearance to the weary smoke-filled eyes of Londoners in the summer, other theatres survived: the Phoenix reopened with a variety season and the Stoll was open for business in July. Suburban houses did well, including the Golders Green Hippodrome where Sarah Churchill was appearing with her husband, Vic Oliver, in *Plays and Music* along with Joyce Carey (Lilian Braithwaite's actress daughter).

A few months later, at the age of twenty-seven, Sarah Churchill joined the WAAF as an aircraftwoman.

Sadler's Wells presented the ballet *Giselle* at the New Theatre in July with Margot Fonteyn and Robert Helpmann; and Glynis Johns played her first 'grown-up' part as the teenage heroine of Esther McCracken's *Quiet Weekend*, a sequel to her earlier success, *Quiet Wedding*.

The main attraction at a railway-workers lunch-time concert in south London was veteran music-hall star George Robey, broadcasting not only to British listeners but to the 'whole Empire'. The critic on the local weekly paper felt it was rather a shame the listeners could only hear the great comedian; they were not able to see his facial expressions or 'the magic use of his right hand serving to punctuate his number, "What Do You Think I Said?"'

The critic went on to praise 'the popular Canadian Troubador Ted Andrews, with Barbara at the piano, who had a wonderful voice and a refreshing style; Barbara was a polished and talented pianist'.

Julie Andrews made her first stage appearance at two as a fairy in Cone-Ripman's Dancing and Drama School, and in 1941 was auditioning as a singing child performer. Two years later she was entertaining in air-raid shelters and appearing with her parents in their music-hall act. Singing at one or two troop shows in London, she came across another child prodigy, Petula Clark, and they 'used to walk around each other with great respect'.

In June Leslie Henson entertained the Royal Princesses, Elizabeth and Margaret who came to a matinée of *Up and Doing* and took tea with him between shows.

With the King and Queen, the Princesses also saw a special showing of the new revue *Black Vanities*, then running at the Victoria Palace. Among the audience were 400 servicemen, stationed near Windsor Castle. The show starred Frances Day, and Flanagan and Allen, and was presented in the Waterloo Chamber at the castle.

One member of the Royal Family not at the revue was Queen Mary. Then in her seventies, she was staying with the Duke of Beaufort at Badminton where she remained throughout the war; writing to friends still in London: 'You've probably noticed that in referring to Italians and Germans I use a small "i" and a small "g". I do this because I dislike them so much.'

A heat wave was reported in July as well as a boom in second-hand clothes. The Board of Trade agreed to give special facilities to theatre people to help them buy stage costumes without having to use their normal clothes ration; they were given an extra sixty-six coupons. Men born between January and June 1900 had to register, including Arthur Askey, then playing at Birmingham. Asked at the exchange if he was drawing unemployment benefit he said, 'No. But I'm willing to try anything.' He didn't feel he'd have to change his job as he was doing his bit keeping up public morale.

By the end of 1941 Basil Dean was able to announce that ENSA was employing just under 2,000 men and women: 'A high proportion of the men were over forty years of age, some of whom were called up, with a likelihood of a greater number of them being required for military service. More actresses were urgently needed for all-women shows as further revues and concert parties along the lines of *Girls in Uniform* were in preparation.'

Around 35,000 films had been shown, and according to ENSA's cinema manager, there were 74 film units in action, giving 500 shows a week: 'As long as we can throw a shadow on the wall, we give 'em a show.' It was announced from Cairo that Naafi's first desert cinema had opened, the first of a circuit of permanent camp cinemas, equipped with a stage and dressing-room accommodation for live ENSA shows.

At home there was a brief respite from bombing over Christmas, and Barbara Mullen was able to open at the Adelphi as *Peter Pan*, with Alastair Sim; Joan Greenwood played 'Wendy' and Zena Dare was 'Mrs Darling'.

Said Barbara Mullen: 'That really was quite a remarkable

experience and I well remember the difficulties when we took the play on tour. It was almost impossible to find men able to work the flying ballet and one night I was flown out into the audience and back on to the stage . . . straight out of the French window. But I loved the flying; to me it's always seemed a perfectly natural way for a human being to travel.

'One night, when I got the cue to fly across the ship, playing my pipes, I realised something at the last moment: I hadn't been hooked on to the wire. I'd to tell Alastair Sim in a stage aside and he whispered back: "What the hell are you going to do?"

'"Hypnotise you!" I hissed and straight away he picked up the cue. He cried out in a loud voice, "Ahah! I'm hypnotised." And then, like the fine actor he was, he promptly jumped over the side of the ship.'

While arrangements were being made to bring American stage and screen stars over to entertain troops in Britain, preparations were started, in November, for an organisation (equivalent to ENSA) in the USA to supply shows to the US army. Barclay S. Leathem, the director of drama at the Western Reserve University in Cleveland, Ohio, planned to present plays and vaudeville to the one and a half million men in the American forces by drawing on performers already in the ranks. He felt 'there was enough talent in the US army to supply the straight theatre with stars for many years to come'.

And two American acrobats, still in London, decided not to return to the States. 'Not on your life. We'd rather face German bombs any day than those New York agents . . .'

You've got to keep moving. You stop in this business,
you're dead

Frank Sinatra, 1942

With the days of real peace almost over there was still a
rainbow cheerfulness about the American theatre in the dark
days of 1941. Midtown Manhattan, the magic blocks that
ran from 34th to 59th Street, was always busy with down-
town theatregoers going through the entertainment section
of *The New York Times*, eager to catch up on new shows,
ready to see old ones the second time around. Some of the
bigger attractions still retain a curiously familiar flavour in
an age of nostalgia.

There were shows such as *Arsenic and Old Lace* at the
Fulton Theatre with Josephine Hull and Boris Karloff;
Lady in the Dark at the Alvin with Gertrude Lawrence, Danny
Kaye and Victor Mature; imaginative musicals like *Cabin
in the Sky* at the Martin Beck with Ethel Waters and
Katherine Dunham, *Panama Hattie* with Ethel Merman at
the 46th Street Theatre and *My Sister Eileen* at the Barrymore
with June Havoc and the inventive Gene Kelly. José Ferrer
was in *Charley's Aunt* at the Cort, and Olsen and Johnson
broke records with their crazy *Hellzapoppin* at the Winter
Garden Theatre.

The film of the year was *Blood and Sand* with Rita

Hayworth, Tyrone Power, Anthony Quinn and, playing a small part, Monty Banks, Italian-born husband of Gracie Fields. And Mickey Rooney was planning to marry a young and pretty brunette called Ava Gardner.

Who knew then that the war zone would suddenly reach from Hollywood to Hong Kong? And that in fifteen months' time New York would be jammed with servicemen on leave and defence workers at play, queueing to see the biggest hit since the original production of *The Merry Widow*? *Oklahoma!* was the musical that wove modern ballet, music and drama into a brand-new style of musical comedy, and it was the first collaborative effort of Richard Rogers and Oscar Hammerstein II. Opening at the St James Theatre on 1 April 1943, with Alfred Drake, Celeste Holm and Howard da Silva, it took its place in the war years alongside the Empire State Building and the Statue of Liberty as one of the city's major attractions.

In 1941, William Saroyan's *The Time of Your Life* won both the Pulitzer Prize and the New York Drama Critics' Award, the first play ever to receive the two honours. The volatile Saroyan (who was to join the US army as a private in the Signal Corps) created more publicity for himself by turning down the Pulitzer Prize on the grounds that wealth should never patronise art, and anyway, all his plays were equally good. As a result, he made five times the amount of money he'd have got by simply accepting the prize.

Towards the end of 1941 a concert was staged at Radio City Music Hall in aid of British air-raid victims. Organised by the American theatre and the British War Relief Society, *Carnival for Britain* was a three-way radio link. From New York, Gracie Fields, Gertrude Lawrence and Burns and Allen were joined by Robert Montgomery, Sir Cedric Hardwicke and Noel Coward broadcasting from Hollywood and by Vivien Leigh, Bea Lillie, Laurence Olivier and Leslie Howard in London.

The latest song was 'My Sister and I', written by two Dutch refugees in America. A best-seller for weeks it overtook in popularity a fragment of lyrical lunacy called 'Hut-Sut Rawlson on the Rillerah', whose double-dutch mock Swedish ditty puzzled many musical experts until a reader of the *Los Angeles Times* sent in an old song sung years before in St Louis night-spots entitled 'Hot-Shot Dawson on a Riverboat', and its authorship was narrowed down to a blind black singer from Missouri who performed it at ferryboat landings around 1914.

It was still the golden age of the big swing bands and on Sunday morning, 7 December 1941 as Americans were listening to hits like Glenn Miller's 'Little Brown Jug' or Benny Goodman's 'Stealin' Apples' or Artie Shaw's 'Frenesi', a news bulletin cut in to announce that Japanese carrier-borne aircraft, supported by submarines, had made a mass attack on the US fleet anchored in Pearl Harbour. The announcement had all the impact of a Hawaiian war club for most Americans, and few realised that with the Japanese contempt for a conventional declaration of war, old codes of honour had gone for good. Unprepared, they found themselves dragged into the whirlpool of a world war and in the space of a few hours the whole pattern of their lives changed.

After the first shock of disbelief America mobilised with long queues surging forward to sign on at army, navy and marine recruiting centres; strikes came to an end and civilians prepared their home defences with blackouts, bomb shelters and air-raid drill.

Two of the first stars to leave Hollywood for the forces were James Stewart and Robert Montgomery (who joined the US Navy and fought at Guadalcanal). Stewart had applied in March 1941 but the army rejected him; while tall and fit, he weighed less than 139lb and was therefore 10lb underweight. Accepted on his second application, he transferred to the Army Air Corps (later USAAF) and by 1943 he was an operations officer in England with a Liberator bomber group. He flew operational trips over Europe and finished the war as a lieutenant-colonel with the American

Distinguished Flying Cross, the Air Medal and French Croix de Guerre.

Other stars joined the navy: Robert Taylor became a naval pilot. Henry Fonda enlisted as an ordinary seaman. At thirty-seven years of age he graduated from Naval Training School, San Diego, as a quartermaster, third class. Commissioned as lieutenant, junior grade, he was made assistant operations officer and played a major role in the central Pacific as air combat intelligence officer to Admiral John Keever, winning a Bronze Star plus a Presidential Citation for his services.

Kirk Douglas and Robert Stack were sailors; also Boston-born Jack Lemmon, who had attended Harvard College. Paul Newman, a student before Pearl Harbour, spent three years as a naval radio-operator in torpedo aircraft flying over the Pacific; Tony Curtis was a signalman. Renowned for his flawless impersonation of Cary Grant, he was able to perfect it while serving on a submarine. For seven months, the crew had just one film aboard, starring Cary Grant, and in the end they knew it so well they used to turn off the sound and do the dialogue themselves.

Curtis was injured loading torpedoes at Guam: 'A chain broke and one end of it cut through the air like a whip and I happened to be in the way. I spent seven weeks in hospital in a very unenviable position indeed with both legs paralysed, but I recovered just in time to see the Peace Treaty signed in Tokio Bay.'

Douglas Fairbanks Jnr, already on the naval reserve, went to sea as a lieutenant and saw service in the Arctic and the Mediterranean as well as participating in the Dieppe raid and Salerno landings. Promoted to Lieutenant-Commander he survived seven major campaigns, twelve amphibious operations and nine months in Combined Operations with Lord Mountbatten. One of the most decorated stars, he won the DSC, Croix de Guerre, Legion d'Honneur and Silver Star.

Lee Marvin was trained to be part of a three-man combat

team, able to infiltrate the haunch and the hump of enemy lines in the Pacific Islands and kill without noise. He demonstrated his toughness and ability in twenty-one landings, including Guadalcanal before being wounded in an ambush. After a year in hospital he was discharged, as hard as teak but with a ten-inch scar across his back.

After the army he studied drama on a service grant with the American Theatre Wing, but finding it difficult to get work as an actor he took a temporary job as a plumber's mate until he got into a repertory theatre; he eventually arrived in Hollywood in 1951.

Aristotle 'Telly' Savalas, the second eldest in a Greek immigrant family living on Long Island, was seriously thinking about a career in professional football until Pearl Harbour came along and then he went straight into the army. Although he was severely wounded, spending two years in an army hospital, all he has to say on the subject is: 'I got hurt in the war and spent a long time in hospital. I underwent hardships, so did a lot of others who didn't come back and I don't care for heroes. Let it go at that.'

Glenn Miller was commissioned as a major and took the American Expeditionary Forces Band to Europe, with Sergeant Broderick Crawford acting as compère. Frank Sinatra, however, was rejected as unfit for military service because of a punctured eardrum, and by July 1944 he was said to be the world's biggest moneymaker, earning £375,000 a year.

With the USA in the war, it was suggested that a number of Hollywood stars might visit Britain and among those named as likely to go were Judy Garland, Bing Crosby, Bob Hope and Deanna Durbin, then married to a junior producer, Vaughn Paul.

From her first film, *Three Smart Girls*, the young soprano was a star and for twelve years every picture she made from *100 Men and a Girl* (with conductor Leopold Stokowski) to *The Butler's Sister* was a box-office success; her records, from hit songs to grand opera, sold in hundreds of thousands;

she divorced Vaughn Paul and married scriptwriter Felix Jackson; still a star, still climbing ... and then suddenly it was all over.

She didn't appear in public for a long time, and marrying French film director Charles David she went to live with him in France, in a house in the Rue de Viviers, Neauphle-le-Château, thirty miles from Paris. Deanna Durbin has visited London in recent years but no one has recognised her.

What made her give up her life as a screen star? 'She wanted to be free,' said David, 'the way she is now and will continue to be. She enjoyed singing but the publicity machine in Hollywood upset her. She wanted a private life. They wouldn't let her have one.'

Her earnings before the war averaged £52,000 a year and it was likely that she was quite prepared to leave the studios for a few weeks to tour Britain. ENSA rashly announced she had agreed to do a four-week tour for them, adding: 'Naturally we'd prefer stars who can do a turn rather than straight actors and actresses and while they will give their services for nothing, we will defray all travelling expenses.' 'Tatler', writing in the *Daily Film Renter*, was a trifle sceptical:

There is a story published far and wide that Deanna Durbin is to come to England. I say it's doubtful we'll see her at any time, let alone before Christmas; and as for those other stars, you won't see any of them during the present hostilities. For one thing, the American government frowns on such things and Universal Studios, since Miss Durbin's contract trouble with them, have put a strict ban on her activities. So don't look for her in the next few weeks.

Despite 'Tatler's' pessimism, all the papers were full of the news of Deanna Durbin's anticipated visit. Then on 24 December her tour was called off. The Hollywood Press dismissed it as 'ballyhoo' meant to scare Universal into settling a three-month-old feud; and the British Embassy in Washington said they intended to issue a statement defending

Miss Durbin's good faith. From her point of view 'the Japanese war upset all her plans' and she wanted the British to know she wasn't afraid to travel, but her husband (the first one) insisted they make the trip together or not at all. Finally, the United States government issued a Press release: 'The Deanna Durbin visit to Europe is off. If she wants to entertain troops there are thousands of them right here.'

In Russia the theatre played an important part in making entertainment accessible to members of its forces: 'Every day', said actress Mademoiselle Knuipper-Chekhova in Moscow, 'we are forming brigades of actors and actresses and sending them off to mobilisation units. This valuable work will continue as long as the German offensive against this country lasts. We are confident eventually of victory.'

In Australia during the winter of 1941 the people were waiting for the first Japanese bombs to fall. Madge Ryan, character actress of considerable distinction, recalls what it was like: 'We expected air-raids any time and as I remember there was precious little to stop them. I'd been acting in Sydney with the Independent Theatre and felt I should do something to help the war effort so I became an ambulance driver. There were a few alerts and some bombs were dropped, and one night I was on duty when Japanese one-man submarines crept into Sydney Harbour. In the middle of all the panic I was silly enough to stop and put on some lipstick before taking the ambulance out. In the end nothing happened and the alert was called off.

'Another time I was living next door to a couple of my husband's relatives and when the siren went I ran in to find two elderly aunts calmly lying on mattresses under the table.

'As an added precaution they had put preserving pans over their heads and rubber plugs in their mouths. They told me the plugs were to prevent their teeth suddenly crashing together if a bomb fell on them . . .

'And three enemy submarines really did fire torpedoes across Sydney Harbour but the only damage reported was shattered windows and the only casualty a cat that died of fright.'

Madge Ryan stayed in Sydney throughout the war, finding plenty of work with the Australian Broadcasting Commission as well as the commercial stations. She also worked in the theatre as places like the Minerva, Tivoli and Theatre Royal all kept going. 'We did plays like *The Little Foxes* and *The Cocktail Party* and I worked with Maggie Fitzgibbon, Bill Kerr, and Peter Finch.'

Peter Ingle-Finch started life in London and did a fair amount of travelling before he dropped the 'Ingle' and became Peter Finch, actor. During the war he spent some time in the Middle East with an anti-aircraft regiment until he was posted to the First Army Theatre, an entertainment unit whose job was to provide relaxation for Australian servicemen stationed in various parts of Africa. 'We found talent among the troops, played in makeshift theatres, mostly in the open air and made do with the minimum amount of scenery. Anyone with a harmonica was a godsend. An accordionist was a miracle.'

Comedian Dick Bentley, the Australian half of the team in *Take It from Here* which ran on BBC Radio from 1948 to 1960 (with Jimmy Edwards), learned to play the violin in Melbourne, worked in musical comedy in Sydney, and did a considerable amount of broadcasting in Australia before arriving in London in 1938 to work for the BBC (although he returned to Australia to work for the forces during the war).

Just before the war he was the Bentley part of 'Moon and Bentley', a double act working for Jack Hylton in *Youth Takes a Bow*. Dick Bentley recalls:

'The youth part in the title applied to a group of little cherubs who made up the first half of the show. Two of them, Eric Bartholomew and Ernest Wiseman, better known today as Morecambe and Wise, said a couple of years ago on television that they started in comedy by modelling themselves on an act called "Moon and Bentley". It's a wonder to me they ever got anywhere at all.

'Soon after the war began I told the Agent General for Victoria that I wanted to go back to Australia to introduce a new kind of radio show for the forces similar to the one being done by the BBC, and he gave me a letter of recommendation ...

'Then the army asked me to go overseas so I took *The Dick Bentley Celebrity Party*, what a bloody awful title that was, on a tour of New Guinea and the Solomon Islands ...

'We were at Madang in New Guinea playing to soldiers who were leaving next day to fight the Japs, and during the second house the neck suddenly parted from my violin, in front of 4,000 servicemen. It stopped the show but it didn't do the violin any good. Next morning I got hold of a carpenter and he put it in a vice but found he couldn't glue it together again without distorting the sound-post. So he sent word around the camp: Did anyone know anything about violins? An LAC turned up who'd worked on them in Glenn's Music Shop, Melbourne, and he knew how to fix it, even in New Guinea.

'Two things stand out from those days: the commander of US naval forces at Bougainville in the Solomons who wrote to the Australian government saying how much he appreciated our show, and the comment of an Aussie soldier when asked his opinion of the Dick Bentley party, "It was *extra*!"'

In January 1942 New York's Tin Pan Alley went to war. According to songwriter Johnny Mercer: 'Irving Berlin took charge, the way he did in World War I and organised *This Is the Army*, a show made up of all serving personnel. I wrote a song called "GI Jive", which was a hit, but I don't think there was any really big song like there was in the first war. Maybe "Don't Sit under the Apple Tree with Anyone Else but Me". That was a great song that everyone could sing and understand its meaning.'

Metronome, the American music magazine, named Frank Sinatra, singing with Tommy Dorsey's band, best male singer of 1941, and *Time* magazine reported him as

> appearing on the stage like a terrified boy in the presence of his first major opportunity. His face was like a wet rag…his chest caved in as if from the weight of the enormous zoot suit shoulders it bore and a huge floppy bow tie hung down like the ears of a spaniel. For a moment he looked among his audience pleadingly as if searching for his mother and then he began, timidly and with trembling lips, to sing.

A bandleader of the 1940s put it more crudely: 'The little jerk really believed those stupid words.' So did the hordes of bobby-soxed, saddle-shoed screaming girls who held up traffic outside New York's Paramount Theatre on 42nd Street at his first solo concert in December. As he stepped on stage to sing with the Benny Goodman band a formidable sound went up, 5,000 teenagers stamping, yelling, applauding; and as he sang the first few words of 'For Me and My Gal', Sinatra, the Voice, the symbol of romance for all the lonely people, the phenomenon, was on his way.

'The most exciting entertainer of our time', now in his sixties, announced his retirement in 1971 and summed up his show-business career as follows: 'It has been fruitful, busy, uptight, loose, sometimes boisterous, occasionally sad but always exciting.'

The American film industry confidently looked forward to 1942, the most prosperous year it had ever known, and box-office takings of outstanding pictures were described by *The Hollywood Reporter* as 'terrific, fabulous and unprecedented with New York Christmas holiday business touching an all-time high'.

The explanation? It was all due to defence spending and the national desire to escape from the grimness of war. *Louisiana Purchase* established a new record at the Paramount Theatre with £23,000 taken in its first week; *Remember the Day* took £25,000 at the Roxy; *Babes on Broadway* £24,000 in five days at Radio City Music Hall and *The Man Who Came to Dinner* £10,000 in four days at the Strand Cinema. The British picture *How Green Was My Valley* did even better business than *A Yank in the RAF*.

On 20 January Carole Lombard, the wife of Clark Gable, was killed in an aircraft crash near Las Vegas on her way back to Hollywood from the first war-bond rally held at her hometown, Fort Wayne, Indiana. The funeral service took place two days later at the Church of the Recessional, Forest Lawn.

On 12 August, forty-one-year-old Clark Gable went to the recruiting office in the Federal Building in Los Angeles and enlisted as a private in the air-force. He didn't want to sell bonds, he said, or make speeches or entertain. He just wanted to be sent where the going was tough. After gunnery training he was commissioned and posted to Biggs Field, Texas, the transit base for the European Theatre of Operations.

From there Lieutenant Gable flew to join 351st Bomber Group at Peterborough, England, and took command of a photo-film unit. He went on his first operational flight as an observer in a B17 on a raid over Antwerp in May 1943 and, completing four more missions shooting colour film during combat, he was recalled to Washington at the end of that year, taking with him over 50,000 ft of film for use in gunnery training. Awarded the Air Medal 'for exceptionally meritorious achievement while participating in five separate missions', Gable was promoted to major and honourably discharged to be placed on the reserve list in June 1944. His order was signed by Hollywood actor Captain Ronald Reagan, USAF Personnel Office, Culver City (the headquarters of the films division of the air-force, formerly the Hal Roach Studio).

Other stars who stayed civilians toured with the United Services Organisation or sold war bonds. USO Camp Shows Incorporated provided entertainment for US servicemen both in the USA and the European Theatre of Operations, with Al Jolson heading the first party to play for GIs in the United Kingdom. Edward G. Robinson was another early arrival, sponsored by the US Office of War Information, and one of the most popular shows was undoubtedly the all-girl party starring Kay Francis, Martha Raye and Carole Landis (who five years later took an overdose of sleeping pills and was found dead on the floor of her Hollywood home).

Basil Dean sailed to New York on the *Queen Elizabeth* for talks with the chairman of USO, only to find that Abe Lastfogel had just left by air ... for London. Dean called in at the Stage Door Canteen and was surprised to see actor Alfred Lunt 'with an apron tied round his middle, helping with the washing-up'; all part of the involvement of American show business in the war effort, with similar canteens set up in the large cities. Actors and actresses playing in these cities gave voluntary service, playing in cabaret and serving snacks to the Allied forces.

In the Hollywood canteen, Bette Davis and Olivia de Havilland danced with servicemen and waited at table, and a victory train set off from Los Angeles en route to Washington with stars like James Cagney, Laurel and Hardy, Cary Grant and Groucho Marx aboard; actresses included Claudette Colbert and Merle Oberon with Marlene Dietrich joining them to meet the president at the White House. The train stopped at towns along the way with the stars parading through the streets before putting on a show in the evening.

The friction that had developed between ENSA and Army Welfare in London was repeated in Washington in the struggle between the Red Cross and USO for the right to entertain troops overseas. It was General Marshall, then Chief of Staff, who settled the argument by allowing USO to control shows overseas, with the Red Cross authorised to present entertainment in their own clubs and hostels in the USA.

The American Theatre Wing (War Service Inc) brought together all branches of stage, screen, radio, vaudeville and music for war service, playing host to more than 3,000 servicemen every night at its canteen on West 44th Street, New York.

Burns Mantle, theatre critic of the New York *Daily News*, felt that 'the theatre in wartime as well as in peace offered a vivid reflection of the way of life that our liberties and opportunities have granted us. It was therefore representative of those liberties and opportunities for which we, as free men, were willing to fight and die. It should be proudly sustained.'

He wrote this in a programme note to a new Emlyn Williams play *The Morning Star* which opened on Broadway with Gladys Cooper, Jill Esmond – and a newcomer with only one previous Broadway appearance 'who did a superlative job with sensitivity and fine restraint as the young doctor'. This was Gregory Peck who had been in *The Doctor's Dilemma* with Katherine Cornell. A native of California, he had been taking a premedical course at the University of Columbia until he changed his mind and chose instead a theatrical career.

Thirty-five years later he decided not to look for acting roles anymore. The moment of truth came for him when, as President of the Motion Picture Academy for Arts and Sciences he had to present a special award to Cary Grant for his services to the cinema: 'It set me thinking; maybe I've done enough myself. And if I don't act again I'll be perfectly happy.

'The high point in a picture comes when it's all over, months later. If the film's a success you get a temporary glow of gratification but it's remote and fleeting. People stop you in the street and say: "I enjoyed that one." It's pleasant but nothing like the applause in a theatre which is immediate. The kind that only happens when you've just shared an experience within the same four walls.

'I expect there'll still be a role that will interest me one day and if it comes along I'll be perfectly happy to do it. If not, well I'll still be perfectly happy working as a producer.'

Shortly after the remnants of the British army in Burma were forced to retreat back into India, the rumbustious Errol Flynn – formerly of the Northampton Repertory company – made the ill-timed *Objective Burma*, the film that simulated the conditions of the Burma campaign on location at the luxurious Santa Anita Ranch in California, and implied that the out-of-tune heroics of Mr Flynn were such that he could well win World War II single-handed.

Reaction to the picture in Britain was quick and angry; people felt strongly about the film actor sitting secure in his Hollywood glasshouse while their soldiers were bleeding and being killed under the most appalling conditions in the worst fighting country in the world.

While aware of the scathing comments in Britain, Flynn was preoccupied with a more serious personal matter. He was the defendant in a double statutory rape charge in Los Angeles.

'Statutory rape' in California was a modification of an earlier law passed to protect young girls, and decreed that a man who had carnal knowledge of a person, or persons, under eighteen years of age was liable to a prison sentence of five years or more, whether or not the person gave her consent.

When the case went for trial, with lawyer Gerry Geisler defending the actor, the court proceedings gained greater space in American newspapers than the current war news. Flynn was concerned with the effect the case would have on his sister Rosemary (ten years younger than he was), and on his father, who was then Professor of Zoology at Queen's University, Belfast. Rosemary had recently become engaged to a newly qualified solicitor and had cabled the news to her brother in Hollywood from their home in Northern Ireland.

Found not guilty, Flynn had to pay over $50,000 in expenses. Another part of the price, as he reflected ruefully in his autobiography—brooding sombrely over the disappointment of pleasures achieved and a life thrown away—

was that 'a new legend was born and a new saying became part of the national idiom . . . A GI or Marine or sailor went out at night sparking and the next day he reported to his cronies, who asked him how he made out, and the fellow said, with a sly grin, "I'm in like Flynn." '

'The company commander came into the hut and asked,
"What's all the filthy language?"
'"It's the sergeant, sir," I said. "He can't find his prayer
book."'
Stars in Battledress *Comedian*, 1942

Terry-Thomas recalls his call-up: 'The blow fell while I was playing Malton with an ENSA company in 1941.

'It seemed that Ernie Bevin – who was responsible for conscription – was engaged in a private war with Basil Dean. Accordingly, to prove how powerful he was, Bevin churlishly decreed that over thirty of ENSA's key chaps had to don khaki or one of the shades of blue.

'This came as a fearful shock because I was one of them ... but there it was, a slight shift in policy and I was converted into cannon-fodder overnight.

'I reported to the Army Signals Depot at Ossett, Yorkshire, struggling manfully with absolutely heaps of personal stuff: fine raiment, false noses, wigs, scripts, guitars and so forth. It didn't go down at all well in the guardroom and when I enquired where I might leave my luggage I was given a short but explicit piece of advice.

'However, succeeding in some degree in tempering the military wrath I settled down and as an antidote to the numbness of everyday routine I put on a show at the local town hall where I tried out my sketch about feet. This was based on all the suggestions about the medicinal treatment of feet torn by the rigours of boots and square-bashing, and I put the lot in; everything from Epsom Salts and vinegar to methylated spirits and a mustard poultice. If you had used them all, your feet would have dropped off. The sketch went over very well and the show was a big success.

'After I was posted to Huddersfield I produced a few more shows in the area and I was doing a Sunday concert at York in a cinema when Captain George Black Jnr, who was in charge of the Central Pool of Artistes, spotted me and sent me to a *Stars in Battledress* unit. After the Cromwellian austerity of Huddersfield, life from then on became positively luxurious.'

A popular unit was a 'Palm Court' type of show with a string sextet, good solo singer, and Terry-Thomas to introduce the numbers:

'Things like selections from *The Merry Widow* or *Czardas* and all the boys used to troop out afterwards as pleased as punch. To their surprise they'd listened to a "classical" concert and enjoyed it. This show gave me a marvellous opportunity to try out a fresh approach to comedy, and around this time I began working on a sketch that was the turning-point. It not only made my name but also a lot of money after the war.

'You remember when the BBC was bombed in 1941 and Bruce Belfrage carried on reading the news? [The wartime newsreader stayed at the microphone as a bomb fell on Broadcasting House, and with only a moment's hesitation continued reading the news until the end.] Well my sketch "Technical Hitch" was all about a BBC announcer who couldn't find the records he was supposed to play so he imitated each one over the air. I'd had the original idea for some years since the night I'd been to see Richard Tauber in *Old Chelsea* and popped into a pub across from the theatre. I heard a disc jockey doing his thing on the radio in the lounge bar . . . and then it happened, the poor chap lost his script or something and became hopelessly mixed up.

'I nursed the idea for over three years and everywhere I went I carried a case full of the records I was going to use but I never unpacked them, Tauber, Noel Coward, Hutch, Eddie Cantor . . . the great thing about those artistes was they all had distinctive styles. It would be far more difficult to imitate most of today's singers.

'Finally I tried out the sketch in front of the army at a concert in Olympia at the end of 1942, no props, simply a table and a chair and it was an enormous success so I gradually built it up from there.'

The first repertory unit of *Stars in Battledress* was formed with Private Richard Hurndall directing *Without the Prince* (in which he had appeared at Coventry before the war) and Clive Brook's daughter, a member of the ATS, was transferred to the Central Pool of Artistes. Faith Brook had studied at RADA until September 1939 when she was evacuated to America and her acting career began with three lines in a film, Alfred Hitchcock's *Suspicion*.

'Then I was cast as an English girl in a play, *Letters to Lucerne* which opened in Boston, Massachusetts, the day after Pearl Harbour was bombed. We ran all of three weeks on Broadway and after we closed American Equity wouldn't allow me to take another theatre job for six months and I just managed to survive doing some radio and bits and pieces of modelling.'

After working in what was known as 'little theatre', the nearest California got to professional repertory, Faith Brook's big chance came with the opening of *Lottie Dundass* at the new Lobero Theatre in Santa Barbara. Charles Boyer saw her in the play and offered her a contract with a production company he was setting up at Universal Studios, but Faith Brook decided instead it was time to head for Britain and put in some war effort.

'I came back and reported to the labour exchange and they asked me what service I wanted to join; when I said the Women's Royal Naval Service they jeeringly told me that was out of the question unless I knew an admiral and said I could have six months' freedom before I was drafted. I applied to join ENSA but on the day the committee accepted me I was told to report to the ATS at Warrington.'

During the six months' grace she played the ingenue in *Aren't Men Beasts?* with Alfred Drayton and Robertson Hare, and the play opened at Bristol to the usual pre-West End build-up; but owing to some trivial misunderstanding the publicity turned nasty and they made her the scapegoat for all the draft-dodgers.

'There were headlines like "Why isn't she in one of the services?" and "Who paid for her trip to Hollywood?" which caused tongues to wag and diplomatic wires to hum. The whole business got out of hand, with questions asked in the House of Commons and I'm sure it must have been to save several faces that I was bundled into the ATS. When my recruit training was over the platoon commander told me the Press were anxious to talk to me, but all they got was an emphatic "No" to the question, "Did I like the army?" and finally I was allowed to transfer to *Stars in Battledress*, being demoted from acting lance-corporal unpaid back to Private Brook, W/261722. I don't have to look the number up . . . it's imprinted on my mind for life.'

The year 1942 was a brisk one for West End theatres, with shows like *Goodnight Children* running at the New Theatre starring Naunton Wayne, Patricia Hayes and George Cole; in *Twenty to One* at the Victoria Palace Lupino Lane was hoping for another big winner, but the most significant opening that year was *The Doctor's Dilemma* at the Haymarket with Vivien Leigh and Irish actor Cyril Cusack (later replaced by Peter Glenville, when he went back to Ireland).

Ivor Brown, then at the peak of his profession as drama critic and editor of *The Observer*, noted that

Vivien Leigh as 'Jennifer' sails exquisitely into the play as if from a Sargent canvas . . . and brings to it all the quick loveliness she has lately bestowed in the film studios on two less reputable beauties, Scarlett O'Hara and Emma, Lady Hamilton. She also brings a singularly clear and gracious diction . . . all the more welcome at a time when the drama is often an unworthy daughter of the mother tongue.

The revue *Rise Above It* celebrated its 350th performance at the Comedy Theatre with Hermione Gingold, Hermione Baddeley, Carol Lynne and Walter Crisham.

Hermione Ferdinanda Gingold, the actress whose distinctive voice has been described as 'sounding like asthma set to music', recalled working in revue during the London blitz, occasionally having to stay in the theatre until the all clear and joining in improvised concerts with the audience: 'Sometimes one of them would come up on the stage and do an act – quite often it seemed as though the front stalls were full of zealous amateurs sitting with bulging music cases biding their time until a raid started so they could have a chance of performing on a West End stage.'

Hermione Baddeley toured the Middle East for ENSA during the war and one ex-serviceman will never forget the night she did a concert at Malta with Walter Crisham. Fred Sheppard sat in the front row as they sang a comedy duet 'Give Me This Rose': 'At the end of each verse, Crisham snatched at the flower she was wearing in her cleavage.

'There must have been yards of stalk attached and he kept tugging at it and singing the last line over and over again until the stalk was spread around the stage . . . she managed to stuff the lot back down her dress before he finished the next verse and then they started the whole thing over again.

'The last verse was slightly different: in exasperation Walter Crisham should have grabbed the rose and her bra, the idea being that two ornate brass cups would be revealed, one on each breast. Things didn't go according to plan that night; in his enthusiasm he pulled the cups off as well leaving Miss Baddeley standing in the middle of the stage . . . topless. Naturally this brought the house down but without faltering for a second she gracefully pirouetted until her back was turned to the audience and she was able to replace the cups. Turning again she bowed to acknowledge the loudest applause I ever heard at an ENSA concert.'

That great lady of the theatre, Marie Tempest, died aged seventy-eight on 14 October 1942, 'a lonely old woman in a world where she increasingly felt herself an alien'. Born Mary Susan Etherington, she had been on the stage since 1885 appearing in musicals, light operas and straight plays. Celebrating her golden jubilee in 1935 with a testimonial matinee at Drury Lane, attended by King George V and Queen Mary, she raised £5,000 which went to endow a 'Marie Tempest Ward' at St George's Hospital, Hyde Park Corner, for the benefit of actors and actresses. She was awarded the DBE in 1937.

Of the more than 350 small blue plaques on buildings which mark the former homes of famous citizens, most of them are dedicated to politicians or writers. There are very few commemorating 'those abstracts and brief chronicles of their time', stage performers, but a plaque was put up in March 1972 to mark the house in Park Crescent, Marylebone, where Dame Marie lived at the turn of the century.

Variety artiste Harry – 'Any Old Iron?' – Champion died on 14 January 1942 soon after finishing a week at a London music-hall and broadcasting in *Happidrome*; Felix Powell, the man who wrote the hit song of World War I, 'Pack Up Your Troubles', was found suffering from gunshot wounds in a wood near Peacehaven, Sussex. He died on 10 February 1942; the verdict was suicide.

Sir Oswald Stoll, seventy-six, died at Putney. Fifty years a music-hall proprietor, both his pantomimes at the Coliseum and Stoll were breaking box-office records – in 1942 the Stoll and the Coliseum were taking £6,000 a week.

A teetotaller and non-smoker, every day of Sir Oswald's life he wore his top hat and frock coat with its high stiff collar on the daily journey from home to his office – until he lost them both in the blitz.

Among memorable births worth recording, to remind us that there is a season and a time to every purpose under heaven, is that of Muhammad Ali (formerly Cassius Clay) at Louisville, Kentucky on 17 January 1942; two days later Michael Dumbell-Smith was born at Salisbury, Wiltshire, shortly after his RAF pilot father was shot down and killed. Educated in London, he was a choirboy at St Paul's Cathedral and he began his professional career as Michael Crawford, boy soprano, in Benjamin Britten's *Let's Make an Opera*.

Bebe Daniels and Ben Lyon had been working with ENSA, playing all kinds of small outposts, some of them dates they visited as a result of requests they received by mail.

'It varied a great deal,' Ben recalled. 'One night we'd play to maybe thirty soldiers and the next night it might have been a factory audience of over 2,000. Eventually I told Bebe it was ridiculous going all over the place at random so why didn't we do something on radio that could reach millions. She sat down then and there and wrote the first script of *Hi Gang*; the BBC read it and gave permission for six shows at a nominal fee and the show—with Vic Oliver—caught on and ran until 1943 when we did a follow-up series, *Bebe, Vic and Ben*.

'*Hi Gang* went out every Sunday night, opening with Bebe's wonderful line, "Welcome everybody to *Hi Gang*! Coming to you from the heart of London." We broadcast the show from Maida Vale studios until they were bombed and then we sent it out from Portland Place; but they wouldn't allow us to have an audience there so we moved once again. Hitler certainly kept us on the go. We also did *Gangway* at the London Palladium for forty-seven weeks until 15 December 1942, when I walked into the London headquarters of the US Air Force to be sworn in. I'd been a qualified pilot since 1928 so that was my natural choice. I like to joke that Errol Flynn and I won the war between us; he took care of the Burma campaign at Paramount while I kept an eye on the European Theatre of Operations.

'Long after the war we got mail from people who'd been living in occupied countries asking was it true all that laughter and gaiety coming from London during the blitz. Their own propaganda was very strong and they couldn't believe it was possible. We found we could create better propaganda simply by injecting a funny line somewhere; it was far more effective than brain-washing. Especially during the blitz, like that old gag about the two cockneys in a top-floor apartment during a raid and as they ran downstairs to the shelter, the wife suddenly turned back. "Where're you going?" shouted the husband, still running.

'"I'm going back for my teeth."

'"Don't be a silly old fool. They're dropping bombs, not ham sandwiches."'

Cairo, as the headquarters of the MEF (Middle East Forces) was naturally the hub of all activities, with vast bases at Heliopolis, Port Said, Alexandria, Ismailia and Suez on the outer periphery. With the large amount of British servicemen stationed there, what was then known as Palestine served as an important auxiliary base.

Sergeant Noel Howlett had arrived in Cairo at the end of 1941 as part of the RASC/Expeditionary Forces Institute attached to ENSA. The major in charge had no idea what to do with him until early in 1942 a unit stationed at Maadi Camp in Cairo staged *Night Must Fall*. By personal order of General Claude Auchinleck, then commanding the British Eighth Army, ENSA was instructed to send the play on a tour of the Egyptian bases and Sergeant Howlett went with it as manager.

'I stayed with *Night Must Fall* until I was recalled to Cairo to be told that ENSA was about to take over broadcasting in the Middle East and I would be in charge. Knowing precisely nothing about running a radio station I was appalled. Fortunately the army had no intention of leaving such a vital instrument for propaganda in the chubby hands of ENSA and Army Welfare took it over.'

Howlett stayed in ENSA's Cairo office doing clerical work until a civilian company arrived from Drury Lane to tour the play *George and Margaret*. He had been in the West End production during its two-year run and knew several of the actors in the company. They were delighted to see him again as they had lost their juvenile lead en route and the play needed a new production.

'"Please," I begged them,' said Howlett, '"tell the major I can produce it for you, and get me out of this office."

'The major sent for me, "Look here, sergeant, ever heard of a play called *George and Margaret*?"

'"Most certainly, sir. I was in the original London production."

'"Now wait a minute," said the major. "I saw the bloody play and I don't remember *you* in it."

'"I played the father, sir."

'"Well I'll be buggered," said the major. "You'd better produce the bloody thing here then."

'As a result of that I became official producer of plays for ENSA in the Middle East and did twelve all told until I sailed home in 1945.'

Among the cast of *George and Margaret* was Barbara Leake, who had left *Quiet Weekend* (then playing Wyndhams Theatre) to join ENSA, Frederick Wheldon, Bay White, Bryan Matheson, sixty-five-year-old May Hallatt and Hazel Hughes. After opening at the Royal Opera House, Cairo, the company went on to play in other Egyptian towns and arrived at Alexandria in time to open the newly built Globe Theatre adjoining the Fleet Club. They played to enthusiastic audiences there for several weeks, until news came through that Rommel's forces were at El Alamein, just two hours by road from Alexandria.

The company was told to pack up everything and stand by to return to Cairo. A Naafi bus drove them across the desert road back to the capital. Early next day the bus set off for Ismailia, stopping on the way at the Continental Hotel to pick up more ENSA artistes including Roma Milne, Hugh

French, Norman Hackforth and Marilyn Williams – the first American to entertain Allied forces in the Middle East; and then they set off in convoy along the Sweet Water Canal towards Lake Timsah and Ismailia.

Hazel Hughes recalled the hurried evacuation (just two weeks before her sudden death in November 1974. Aged sixty-one, her last part had been as the daily help in the West End revival of Coward's *Private Lives* with Vanessa Redgrave at the Phoenix Theatre).

'A curfew was imposed once the Germans were fifty miles from Alexandria, and Barbara Leake and I went to the theatre that night to tell the boys there'd be no show. Then we went back to the hotel and had a party with lots of army friends we knew we might never see again. When we were called out at dawn to leave for Mecca or somewhere we felt like hell and to make everything worse May Hallatt threw a temperament: "Well I'm not leaving Alexandria," she said. "I'm having a new set of false teeth made here with transparent tips on them and I'm certainly not going without them." She didn't realise how serious it was and of course she had to come with us.

'The extraordinary thing about that particular flight out of Egypt was that once we all arrived at Ismailia we were told we had to join the army. The ENSA men became soldiers and the girls were put into the ATS along with the other ENSA personnel already there.

'We were bedded down in tents and fell asleep to the sound of gunfire from Suez where German aircraft were laying mines. Early next morning the whole motley crowd of us, including Alice Delysia, piled into buses and moved out of the town across the Sinai Desert towards Palestine. We stopped for lunch somewhere like Bir Rod Salima or it might have been Abu Aweiqila and were given loaves of bread and bully beef; this was washed down with warm water and we were off again. Still on the road at midnight, we were all shivering with cold, we were still wearing civilian undies below the battledress.

'Then about two in the morning one of the lorries broke down, on the side of a mountain. It was daybreak before we reached the top and began going down the other side. Half-an-hour later we passed Jaffa and all I could see in the distance were crumbling white stone walls and what seemed like miles and miles of orange trees and then someone looked out of the bus window and said, "Oh look, Jerusalem". And there it was, shining in the morning sunlight.'

Noel Howlett takes up the story: 'It began to look as though the Germans were going to overrun Egypt and the army issued an order forbidding the evacuation of civilians; they wanted to avoid having all the roads jammed with fleeing refugees so an officer hit on the solution: "Swear all the ENSA artistes into the army and then they could be shifted to Palestine." They were all sworn in and issued with uniforms at Ismailia, all except Alice Delysia who had her own uniform in a becoming shade of blue, covered in Free French insignia.

'Somehow or another in the confusion all the records of these people disappeared and no one knew that they had joined the army. *George and Margaret* simply went on with their tour and played Jerusalem and Tel Aviv before going on to Jordan and Syria. They gave a final performance in the Zion cinema at Jerusalem and then the company split up.'

'Do you know,' said Avril Angers, 'apart from playing in pantomime at Dudley one Christmas I was with ENSA until 1944?'

Before sailing to the Middle East she was in an ENSA show at Portsmouth and a naval officer made a point of speaking to her in the wardroom afterwards. He asked what her future plans were and she told him about the overseas tour. 'What a shame,' he said, 'you'd have been ideal for a production of mine that's shortly going into the West End.'

'And that's how I first met Vivian Ellis. We corresponded for some time and eventually worked together on Leslie Henson's *Gaieties*; he wrote me a song that was a send-up of Frances Day's "It's Delicious, Delightful, De-lovely". Mine was called, "It's Disgraceful, Disgusting and I Didn't Like It".

'Our first port of call in the Middle East was Freetown, West Africa, which seemed at first glance to be one big coaling station and the bottom of everything. ENSA was brand-new out there and Army Welfare, who had been presenting concerts, resented us coming out right in the middle of their quarrel with Drury Lane. To them we were neither fish nor fowl, nor even birds in the hand.

'It was simply a case of the poor bloody actors falling between two feuds... but at least we were billeted in officers' quarters and given some native boys as batmen and they didn't give a damn who we were. Six of us girls shared a room and a native boy known as "Tomato". He called each of us "Sir". Naturally there were certain difficulties as a result of this arrangement.

'For instance, our singer Gloria was stripped to the buff one morning trying to have a wash-down in a small enamel basin when in strolled Tomato – I don't think we *appealed* to him or anything like that; he didn't really fancy us if you know what I mean. Gloria, always the soul of modesty, shrieked and grabbed a towel while I tried to explain to our boy about knocking on the door and waiting until someone said "Come in". I mimed it, he bowed and I said "Knock!" He nodded his little woolly head and smiled and said, "Yes, sir!"

'Act Two: the next morning, same set, same cast: Gloria at her ablutions, awesomely naked and in came Tomato. He crossed over to Gloria in what one might reasonably call a pregnant silence and stared at her body for a moment or two before turning around and going back to the door. He then knocked loudly on the inside, shouted "Come in!" and walked to the centre of the room where he stopped, bowed and said, "Thank you, sir".

'Apart from the bloody climate, another hazard in West Africa was a strange kind of amnesia. On our opening night there, the curtain went up and we all burst on the stage exuding goodwill, full of beans and professional confidence, and got nothing, a complete and dismal silence. That threw us until we realised they liked the show but the pace was too fast and everything had to be slowed down like an action replay. They'd all been out there so long, it was impossible for them to react quickly to anything.

'And I can tell you, after six months we were pretty slow ourselves. Someone might start to say something at the luncheon table, a glazed look would come into their eyes and the sentence would trail off into nothing and never be completed. I'd hate to try and write a book out there; even keeping a diary was out of the question.'

When Nigel Patrick arrived at Geneifa in Egypt he was told by the unit commandant that, at twenty-nine, he was too old to be a reinforcement officer and he was given command of Headquarters company which consisted of five soldiers; a few days later 800 troops descended on the base and it was up to Patrick to find some entertainment for them.

'Even as late as 1942, although both ENSA and *Stars in Battledress* were out there they either never arrived on time or else they'd go to the wrong location.

'I deplored this state of affairs and wrote a series of letters of complaint which found their way to GHQ (General Headquarters); they sent for me and said: "You seem to know something about this business. You'd better go to ENSA and try to put things right." Going first of all to the Canal Zone I immediately insisted, to the fury of the artistes, that all ENSA companies played twice nightly. When I pointed out that if they did ten performances a week instead of six they could have each weekend free they were delighted. That way they were able to get back to the piquant pleasures of Cairo more often; it was only a camel's lope from Ismailia.'

Posted to Algiers, Nigel Patrick was given the job of providing services entertainment for the entire Allied forces in North Africa and southern Europe – apart from Malta and Gibraltar – and he was able to build up an effective organisation: 'The only flaw was Army Welfare. They were still trying to make their mark, and if there were good reports on an ENSA show they implied it was solely as a result of their efforts. Any rubbish, on the other hand, was big bad ENSA's responsibility.

'There were other difficulties. For example I was never informed when troopships were due in port, and I had to find out by devious means through old friends and make sure some kind of entertainment was available. And I begged Welfare to send more shows to the forward areas – there were eleven companies hanging about in Naples most of the time. They could and should have sent much more stuff forward.

'After the Allies invaded Italy in 1943 my "parish" was extended to cover Italy, Greece, Corsica and Sardinia and we worked closely with USO as ENSA had much more live entertainment out in the Middle East than they did. We were also responsible for the film division and at the peak of our time there we had 34 theatres, 131 cinemas and over 3,000 Italians employed by ENSA. When I was due for demobilisation Basil Dean asked me to stay on, and I believe the idea was for Jack Hawkins to handle ENSA throughout the Far East while I would be responsible for anything west of Suez. But I was anxious to get home.'

In those wartime days you could be in the audience one week, and acting on the stage the next. The following is a programme note from the Mercury Theatre in 1944:

FORWARD PLEASE

You may be a lance corporal in your camp but in the MERCURY THEATRE you can be a knight in shining armour one week and a flashing pirate the next. You've always wanted to act, haven't you? Come and try. We also need technicians and dressmakers – in fact everyone from a chimney sweep to a tea taster.

The theatre, situated in Alexandria, was the headquarters of the No 2 Field Entertainment Unit, with Martin Benson as director, assisted by Arthur Lowe.

Lowe was stationed at Quassasin in the Canal Zone, but

after El Alamein he was sent on to Palestine with a detachment of the Royal Army Ordnance Corps: 'It was at the depot at Rafah on the Gaza Strip where the theatre stuff really started...

'It was a desolate place with no diversions of any kind – apart from getting as high as a kite on canteen beer – and a few of us decided to do something about it. The crunch came when in the middle of our plans certain local arab dignitaries pinched all the radios, completely cutting Rafah off from all contact with the outside world. Fortunately it was a simple matter to build a receiver and we also rigged up a loudspeaker system in the Naafi, the focal point of all social life, to broadcast the news every night. Our one record, Glenn Miller's "At Last", became our signature tune and it still makes me nostalgic whenever I hear it.

'The chaps used to queue up just to hear our broadcasts, and this led to our presenting some live shows, making all the scenery, lighting and costumes ourselves. I even wrote to Cairo asking for one-act plays, and my only previous theatrical experience had been in the usual school amateur efforts. Until I went back to the Canal Zone, Tel-el-Kebir this time, I produced and acted in most of the plays and enjoyed every minute of it.'

At Tel-el-Kebir Arthur Lowe again felt the stage under his feet when he appeared in a station revue, and as a result of his success he was seconded to Cairo to work with Edward Stanley who had formed a dramatic group with both civilians and service personnel.

'We were able to present a George Bernard Shaw festival', recalls Arthur, 'with a great cast that included Torin Thatcher and John Arnett. Then Torin Thatcher devised a scheme with the co-operation of Army Welfare to supply service entertainment to the services apart from ENSA. I was promoted to sergeant and posted to Almaza outside Cairo to help him. It worked like this: We'd go out into the desert and encourage troops in isolated units to form their own play groups and concert parties, instructing them in the rudiments of scenery construction and prop making and if any unit wanted to form a band, we'd send them all the musical instruments they needed. We went all over the place and it worked very well. Then while I was at Beirut, my officer, Kenneth Fraser, was sent home to be demobbed and he was replaced by Captain Martin Benson.

'We were posted to Alexandria where he bent a few regulations and transformed a large room over Pay Corps Headquarters into the Mercury Theatre. I think Martin agreed with George Eliot's saying that "it's them as take advantage that gets advantage in this world", and it was surprising how quickly we were able to establish a good solid company. The seating was supplied by the local Workshops for the Blind, and some of the cast were in the army; others were part of the English civilian population and there was also a sprinkling of ATS girls and Wrens.

'We virtually lived in that little theatre and although Martin was on the mat for breaking the rules, he put up a very good case and even got Army Welfare to sponsor us as No 2 Field Entertainment Unit.

'My first job after I came out of the army was with a repertory company at Hulme Hippodrome, Manchester; we did twice nightly and with that kind of experience you either learned the business thoroughly or you got out. After about a year of that we joined Derek Salberg's company at the County Theatre in Hereford in 1947 . . . and inevitably came to London to start the rounds. Looking back I suppose I just progressed gradually and steadily. I was in some of the musicals like *The Pyjama Game* and *Call Me Madam* and *Pal Joey*, and then came "bit" parts in pictures, the first one was *London Belongs to Me* and the first West End play was *Larger Than Life*. I found that because I was a character actor there were always parts available for me.

'Oddly enough it was never my ambition to be a star; I simply wanted to be the best character actor going, but stardom obviously came through television. I don't think I'd have done it without television.'

Jack DeManio first began broadcasting in the Middle East with the Forces Broadcasting Unit in Palestine. He had rejoined the Royal Sussex Regiment in the Sudan in time to fight the Italians at Keren, and nearly lost his leg after getting a bullet just below the knee. He got out of hospital and was posted to the 1st Battalion in the Western Desert, going to Cyprus with them to train for the Battle of El Alamein.

His battalion chased the Germans all the way up to Tunisia and then had to control 80,000 prisoners. When they left for Italy, Jack DeManio stayed on in Egypt.

'A cousin of mine was one of the first broadcasting people in the Middle East, running a service from Beirut and this was expanded under Colonel Dickie Meyer (formerly of Radio Normandy and Radio Luxembourg) who had been sent over to organise the Forces Broadcasting Unit. I was introduced to Meyer and first began broadcasting in Palestine; later on we were based mainly in Beirut.

'None of us knew much about the game and we were looked on as jacks-of-all-trades; if a transmitter broke down we'd all go out and repair it. We had quite a good library of records, one or two ex-broadcasters from Radio Normandy and a couple of others, amateurs like me, who tried to imitate BBC announcers.'

He joined ENSA briefly for a tour of *The Importance of Being Earnest*, produced by Eric Berry with Megan Latimer, Jean Walker and Victor Woolf: 'Eric Berry had fired one of the other chaps in the company because he was always drunk and he asked me to play the part in Palestine for them. I'd known Jean Walker before and she tried to teach me the lines but it was no good, I couldn't remember them and I just couldn't do it properly. The rest of them were awfully good.

'Another actor I remember who used to broadcast from Beirut was Tony Viccars. He was the poor chap who fell out of an hotel window and landed thirty feet on the concrete below, breaking his back, his pelvis, and one of his arms amongst other things.

'We had a lot of fun out there: I remember once I rode a

donkey into the studio while Patricia Ainley and some other actor were doing a request programme and naturally they were rather upset. Another time I borrowed a horse from a Gharry-driver and rode it up the steps and into the Club Excelsior in Alexandria; the poor beast skidded all over the place amid a great deal of laughter, but I managed to get it down again and return it to the owner. I tipped him a quid so he was quite happy about it. I even tried to ride a bicycle into a club at Nicosia but they threw me out. I was always keen on riding in those days; perhaps because I'd been in a mounted regiment in the Territorials.

'I got back to London in 1946 armed with a dozen or so letters of introduction from John Davenport [later chairman of *Reader's Digest* in Britain] whom I'd met in Cairo. I rang up the BBC on 8 February and started work four days later. If I tried that today, I wouldn't get in. It's all specialised nowadays.'

Knowing Egypt as a tourist is one thing, but being there as a serviceman in wartime is quite another. Cairo and Alexandria were the dominant towns for forces on leave. Officers had their own club in Cairo facing the Nile on Sharia Hod el-Laban complete with bedrooms, officers' shop, Old English Bar and a dinner-dance nightly. A certain number of bedrooms were reserved for officers of the women's services. They could visit the renowned Groppi Rotunda for a traditional tea dance, and buy a new uniform from Hamdy Aly in Sharia Adly Pasha.

Jolley's coaches would take them on tours to Luxor, Aswan or Syria from the head office in Sharia Soliman Pasha, opposite the Victory Club. Another rendezvous for officers was Shepheard's Hotel, and the Continental-Savoy was right in the centre of things, overlooking Opera Square and Ezbekia Gardens. They could visit the Khan-el-Khalili market and watch local craftsmen making camel saddles, copper trays and other souvenirs; and if they wished to escape the noise of the streets, there was always a mosque nearby where they could sit quietly and watch the faithful prostrate themselves as they faced Ka'ba at Mecca.

For other ranks, Naafi ran a services shop at Sharia El Fadl, opposite the National Hotel, where troops could buy 'Oriental gifts, Smokers' requisites and Ladies' Toilet Goods'. Women in the services had their own Naafi club at Midan Soliman Pasha with squash bar, showers and ironing-board available. There was a dinner-dance every Tuesday and Thursday where they could dance to the music of Massik's Melody Makers for 15 piastres (15p) apiece.

'In 1942,' said fan dancer Maisie Griffiths, 'I was touring the Orkney and Shetland Islands with Bobby Hind's band. I remember when we were playing aboard some of the naval ships a notice was sent round saying the ladies must wear slacks not skirts. Apparently the boatmen who carried us from the quayside to the ships were getting erotic thrills from seeing suspenders and stocking-tops when we climbed up the ladders.

'We returned to Drury Lane to refit and I was given a message to report to Rex Newman [in charge of the concert parties]; he asked me to go to the Orkneys and I told him I'd just got back.

'"I slipped up there," he said. "How about the Middle East then?" I was given all the inoculations in one afternoon, did a very shaky show at Windsor Castle, and caught a train to Liverpool to board the *Monarch of Bermuda* which took me to Africa. I played some hospitals in South Africa, but there was never a piano available in any of them so we were given an accordionist which wasn't much use to me because I was doing mostly "classical" dancing at the time. Anyway I compromised, bought a couple of fans and also added the can-can to my act, and that was a great hit with the troops – I didn't dance *that* in slacks . . .

'I became an ENSA "lease-lender", switching from one company to another; if anyone fell ill they sent for me and I worked in the sketches as well as doing my own routine and this way I travelled all the way up the Western Desert to Tripoli. It got so that if I found a company I liked I stayed with them as long as I could, otherwise I got out fast.

'It was General Montgomery's idea to send very small units to play the out-of-the-way camps and we'd sleep in all sorts of places, mostly under canvas; working in portable theatres rigged up in a mess hall or canteen.

'From Tripoli I went all the way back down the desert, playing Mersa Matruh, Derna, Tobruk and Benghazi, and over as far as Tel-Aviv. The coach taking us back to Cairo broke down near Heliopolis and while we were standing around in the road wondering what to do a great big black limousine drew up close to us and stopped. It was King Farouk and he gave instructions to his driver to pick up the girls and leave the men where they were. We ignored this and bundled the men in with us. He never spoke a word to anyone on the way into Cairo.'

A few years later the unfortunate Farouk was bundled aboard his yacht *Mahroussa* and sent into exile by an Egyptian army officer called Sadat who had plotted against the British during the war and was given two years in prison for spying. After the war his old friend from army cadet days, Gamal Abdel Nasser, helped him get his commission back.

Hugh F. Berry was in the Desert Air Force and attached to the cinema section of ENSA: 'After initial training in Cairo I became "operational" when the Battle of Alamein began on 23 October, and we managed to give the lads a film show every night with only one day off once a fortnight.

'Once Alamein got going it was a solid push right out of Africa. We followed the army, through Tripoli and up to Tunis where we had the Germans in a pocket on the coast. That night we showed a film while the pocket was illuminated by flares, lit to prevent the enemy from escaping into the sea.'

At home, Jack Hylton presented the previous year's (1941) pantomime success, *Jack and Jill*, with the same cast in a different theatre, His Majesty's; it had run for fifteen weeks at the Palace. Florence Desmond, starring with Arthur Askey, remembered the Queen and the two Princesses coming to a matinée: 'Arthur Askey and myself were taken to their box afterwards to be presented. We were told it was the Princesses' first visit to the theatre for over two years, but they had produced their own *Cinderella* at Windsor Castle, with Princess Elizabeth as Prince Charming and Princess Margaret as Cinderella. The Queen told us. "I'm afraid the jokes were a little old in that show." They all joined the audience in singing a chorus of "Hey, Little Hen" during the matinée.'

'I am disturbed to learn that ENSA is now at Malta. Don't you think the people on that island have been through enough?'
Letter in Newspaper from Serviceman's Wife, May 1943

It was obvious by the beginning of 1943 that there wasn't enough entertainment to go round. There were hundreds of thousands of servicemen, and women, stationed all over the countryside, sometimes billeted near towns but as often located in isolated units beside an anti-aircraft gun or a searchlight, and for most of them the long winter nights offered boredom and very little else. ENSA did what it could, but the sheer bulk of the potential audiences had become too much for the organisation.

While ENSA itself was unwilling to concede this, the absence of any active service member on its central committee was noted by Army Welfare.

One officer said he'd like to 'take the bloody committee, issue them with a hut and a ludo board and tell them: "All you've got to do is keep your chins up and your heads down and there'll be an ENSA production of an outdated version of *East Lynne* along in a few weeks time."'

The flaw in his suggestion was that as the committee consisted of people like Dame Sybil Thorndike, Will Hay and Leslie Henson, they'd have been well able to organise any entertainment they wanted.

144

The practical solution proved to be that the army encouraged units to form their own concert parties. One successful attempt resulted in the formation of *The Four-by-Twos*, a show that consisted of twelve to fifteen soldiers who toured other camps for two months, carrying their own curtains, lights and costumes; a stage-manager visited each camp a few hours in advance to arrange a suitable hall. He also 'borrowed' as many topical jokes as he could for the comedian to use during the performance.

The evening's entertainment began with music from a former professional pianist who accompanied two untrained singers and a ukelele player obviously influenced by George Formby; they were followed by two hefty female impersonators wearing army boots who shook the floorboards in an alarming fashion with their opening dance, and an ageing baritone who assured his audience that Old Father Thames would continue to roll along down to the winding sea. Then came the sketch which described in intimate detail how a country parson and his wife handled a nasty little lot of evacuees and lastly, topping the bill, the comedian:

'There was this sergeant and he said to his squad: "Any of you men know anything about shorthand?" Six recruits stepped smartly forward.

' "Right turn!" ordered the NCO. "They're very short-handed in the kitchen."

'And did you hear about the letter ENSA sent to the Ministry of Labour? "We shall be glad if you will allow us to retain this man a little longer. He is the only male left in a particular company and he is carrying on with fifteen girls . . . " '

He finished his act with several local gags, mentioning the guardroom gigolo or the Naafi nymphet, and everyone joined in the closing chorus of 'We Don't Know Where We're Going Until We're There'. The show was received with thunderous applause; the enthusiasm of the amateur artistes only outweighed by the uncritical approval of the audience.

ENSA artistes, on the other hand, found their audiences harder to please. According to one musician: 'It certainly wasn't all beer and blanket exercises. There were lots of snags ... like a comic finding all his jokes falling flat because an army comedian had used the same material a few weeks earlier, or a singer trying to put over the numbers a little ATS soprano had sung the week before and they had to watch their choice of songs. For example, it wasn't a lot of good singing "If I Only Had Wings" to a hospital audience full of amputees ... But the worst hazard was being in the same company where the manager was having it off with the blonde soubrette who had a jealous husband in the forces. Fraught with tension, that sort of situation, especially when the husband came home on leave unexpectedly.'

An allegation was made that audiences at ENSA shows were sometimes locked in the theatre as a means of making them sit through the whole performance. It was the actor Anthony Verney who had said he personally knew of cases where troops had been locked in a hall to listen to classical music. ENSA, naturally, hotly denied the accusation although it was admitted that there had been occasions when armed guards were posted at exit doors, but only during the invasion scare.

Air-raids on London began again on 17 January 1943, and the Bishop of London presided over a Public Morality Council; out of 366 theatres visited by the Council, thirteen shows 'were open to criticism', and there was complete condemnation of nudity on the stage and a system which permitted lust, blackmail and degeneracy to be portrayed in the guise of entertainment.

ENSA concerts were also 'the cause of grave disquiet' as the Council had received a number of complaints about the jokes used in the shows. A member of the Council, the Archdeacon of Chesterfield, said that the practice of instructing recruits in the use of 'prophylactics' suggested that anti-social behaviour was being adopted as normal ... 'but the modern soldier doesn't take immorality for granted. His resentment of dirt in entertainment demonstrated that quite clearly.'

In the spring of 1943 Leslie Howard prepared to fly to Portugal to lecture for the British Council; he also planned to go on to North Africa to entertain troops. Laurence Olivier decided to film *Henry V* at Powerscourt in Ireland, and Vivien Leigh left for Gibraltar and Algiers.

Miss Leigh went out with an ENSA show, *Spring Party*, that included Bea Lillie, Dorothy Dickson, Mae Craven, Kay Young (Michael Wilding's first wife) and Leslie Henson. The company were in Gibraltar when they heard that Leslie Howard's aircraft had been shot down on the return journey from Portugal on 1 June.

Born Leslie Howard Steiner, he was the son of a stockbroker's clerk Ferdinand Steiner who married Lilian Blumberg. Leslie was born in 1893 and after working briefly as a bank clerk he joined the army at the beginning of World War I and became interested in the theatre while serving in the forces. His wartime film successes included *Pimpernel Smith* and *The First of the Few*, and another picture about the nursing profession, *The Lamp Still Burns*, was released shortly after his death.

As part of a tour of the Middle East, Noel Coward visited Malta and Gibraltar. He gave shows at Malta at naval and military hospitals and then visited the wards of the wounded from Sicily who were unable to leave their beds to see his performance.

He saw *Spring Party* in Gibraltar 'with Bea Lillie giving the most spectacularly brilliant show I had ever seen: it tore the place up'. While the company were having tea with him at the Rock Hotel, discussing the tragedy of Leslie Howard's death, an army officer came over and told them Owen Nares had died suddenly while touring in the play, *The Petrified Forest*, for the troops.

Constance Cummings was in the play and recalls: 'We

opened in Brecon and Owen visited the birthplace of Mrs Siddons, an inn known as 'The Shoulder of Mutton'; he apparently signed his name in the visitors' book and simply collapsed.

She recalls: 'I suppose his heart wasn't too good but none of us knew about it at the time. It was a very hot, close kind of day and I decided to stay in the hotel garden and do some sewing while he went off with a couple of the others from the play. We finished the week with Douglas Jeffries playing Owen's part and then we abandoned it. It was dreadful going on without him.'

The cast of *Spring Party* went on to Tunis and Tripoli to meet General Montgomery, and they found little to do in Tripoli apart from strolling along the palm-bordered promenade close to their hotel, the Italian-owned Albergo del Mehari, or visiting the *Uaddan*, a large mansion on the sea-front being run as a rest centre for officers. Well-furnished bedrooms were available there for the equivalent of 10p a night, and a four-course dinner cost 5p; the charge making up for extras used outside the officers' normal rations.

The basis of each meal was in fact bully beef, so cleverly disguised by the Italian chef that it was hardly recognisable.

When Leslie Henson arrived with the company in Cairo he found Basil Dean awaiting them; Henson lunched in the roof-top restaurant at Shepherd's Hotel with Princess Aly Khan, and was delighted to realise she was 'dear darling Denise Orme's daughter'.

Dean joined *Spring Party* aboard a transport ship with 800 men waiting on deck for the show, and during the interval he sent a message round to the stage-manager: 'Will Mr Henson realise this is a very big ship and please speak up?'

Henson felt this was the last sort of advice he wanted from 'Bas-el-Din': after all his years on the stage he thought he had learned a little about voice projection.

Noel Coward stayed in Gibraltar entertaining and doing a little socialising. According to Henson, 'Coward was visiting one hospital on the Rock, going from bed to bed, sympathising with the wounded and telling the troops he had, in the past, suffered most of the complaints they were then enduring. As he left the surgical ward a voice from the last bed called out: 'I can't wait 'til he gets to the VD ward!'

In October 1943 the USA informed the British Ministry of Labour that USO Camp Shows were the sole organisation responsible for the provision of entertainments for US troops in Britain, and Irving Berlin's *This Is the Army* arrived in London for a service tour.

In authorising an overseas tour for the revue, General George C. Marshall, Chief of Staff US Army, imposed two stipulations: first, soldiers of the Allies as well as American enlisted men should see the show free of cost; second, all money realised from the tour of the United Kingdom should go to British service charities.

Every man in the cast was an enlisted soldier, and the production was directed by Berlin who was also in the show.

He sang 'Oh How I Hate to Get Up in the Morning', the number he had written and introduced in his World War I show *Yip Yip Yaphank* while he was a sergeant stationed at Camp Upton, Yaphank, New York. The original cast of *This Is the Army* when it opened on Broadway on 4 July 1942 included Burl Ives, Ezra Stone, Jules Oshins and Gene Kelly's brother Fred who later became a well-known Broadway dancer. In the film of the show, as well as Captain Ronald Reagan and Sergeant Joe Louis, the stars were Frances Langford, Dolores Costello and the singer Gertrude Niessen.

After a short season at the Palladium, *This Is the Army* toured Italy, Algiers and Northern Ireland where it opened at the Opera House, Belfast, on 13 January 1944.

On 4 November 1943 Evelyn Laye, Dennis Noble and Tommy Trinder, with a revue *Fancy Meeting You*, had a great reception as the first professional entertainment for 750 repatriated prisoners-of-war at a convalescent centre. Miss

Laye was able to talk to a corporal who had written to her from his prisoner-of-war camp in Germany. During the same week the British première of Robert Sherwood's play *There shall Be No Night,* with Alfred Lunt and Lynn Fontanne, took place at the Court Theatre, Liverpool. By arrangement with ENSA and CEMA, servicemen were able to see the first night without charge for admission.

Also in November, the following appeared in the *Empire News*

As bombs showered down on London, two children, brother and sister, played a game of theatre in an air-raid shelter close to a block of flats.

The game developed and soon they were giving nightly performances. Other shelters asked for them and they did a 'tour' on tube trains, giving performances at every station along the way.

Their father, a barber who numbered clients like Ben Lyon and Tommy Trinder among his customers and who lived at Colberg Place, north London, was besieged with requests for their services . . .

In 1943 they were well on the way to professional success. Joyce Blair did a charity show at the Coliseum with Sam Browne and Issy Bonn, and her brother Lionel was in *The Wizard of Oz.* He was later booked by Emlyn Williams for a part in *Watch on the Rhine*; and he also played Jonathan in a radio play, *David and Goliath.*

'We used to shelter in Manor House Underground station,' said Joyce Blair, 'and the atmosphere there was very competitive; a case of who had the finest blankets and the smartest siren suits, with all the mothers trying to out-do each other with the latest fashions. If you set off early enough you got a good place to sleep and you'd settle down there for the night. It was a wonderful social evening, all chatting about the war, husbands coming to have supper before going on duty as wardens or fire watchers, people boarding and leaving trains, and there was always someone who played an accordion.

'Eventually Lionel and I danced and did an act on every station on the Piccadilly line – Finsbury Park, Wood Green, even the West End at Leicester Square. We were invited everywhere, to entertain at parties and weddings.

'Then Lionel became a professional and after playing in London he went on tour and did a season later on at Stratford-upon-Avon, just about the time the doodle-bugs started.'

Faith Brook was in the *Stars in Battledress* production of *Flare Path* doing mostly one-night stands all over the Southern Command 'with a good cast that included Wilfred Hyde-White, Griffith Jones and Kenneth Connor.

'Occasionally an alert would sound in the middle of the play, and the entire audience would disappear; and as soon as the all clear went they'd come back and we'd start again where we left off. We travelled with all the scenery and props and had to put it up and strike it ourselves, as well as packing and unpacking all the props. To speed the whole process at the end of the show we organised it to a fine art. During the last act each of us would take some article or other off as we exited, so that by the time the final curtain came down there was nothing left onstage but the set and the heavier furniture, and we were able to scurry off for a drink in the mess or Naafi canteen.'

In December the Overseas Broadcasting Service, in conjunction with ENSA, made use of foreign stations in Allied hands to give troops a programme of entertainment from home. The recording sessions were part of a nationwide schedule arranged by Army Welfare, which, in 1943, included fourteen touring plays from the central pool of artistes. Plays like Terence Rattigan's *Flare Path* and other West End successes were toured regularly, produced by serving soldiers and played by soldiers and ATS girls for the army.

The broadcasting service was run by Major Basil Brown,

a former company director with theatre interests, and Major Jack Hargreaves, late of the Royal Tank Regiment, who also produced the shows.

When Jack Hargreaves arrived at Southern Television's Southampton studios in 1959 he simply intended to present four programmes called *Gone Fishin'*. He has been there ever since, and is now Deputy Controller of Programmes as well as bringing the simple joys of the countryside to millions with his *Out of Town* programmes, and his regular appearances on the children's television programme *How*.

Before World War II he worked as a writer, first in Fleet Street and subsequently for London Film Productions, Ealing Studios and sound radio. Joining the Royal Artillery in 1940, he transferred to the Royal Armoured Corps on the last day of 1941. He was sent to Sandhurst and commissioned into the Royal Tank Regiment.

'Some time later,' recalled Jack Hargreaves, 'I was appointed to General Grover's staff where I had quite a bit to do with the policy and planning of army radio, particularly for Europe. This developed under a branch of SHAEF [Supreme Headquarters, Allied Expeditionary Force; established in London early in 1944 under General Eisenhower in preparation for D-Day].

'In other commands the same activity developed: in Italy under Colonel Gale Pedrick who later was attached to the War Office; in Cairo under Colonel Richard Meyer [one of the founders of Independent Television]; in India under Major Cave-Brown-Cave; in Baghdad under Major Jack Dibb from the *Yorkshire Post*, and others.'

Lieutenant-Colonel Gale Pedrick Harvey was once a radio journalist and author of the most successful play on radio in 1942, *The Fingers of Private Spiegel*. He was posted to Algiers in November 1943 with Major Emlyn Griffiths, a former West End producer and manager who had been briefly engaged to Heather Jenner at the start of the war, and Major Philip Slessor the BBC announcer. Assisting with broadcasts in Algiers were Captain Andy Gray (who was working with

Major Hugh Cudlipp, Editor-in-Chief of the army news-paper *Union Jack*) and Captain Dick Richards (journalist on the *Daily Mirror*).

On 7 January the experimental broadcasting service opened at a requisitioned French school in Algiers with Leslie Henson and Tommy Trinder starring in the first transmission. The station had a radius of fifty miles; its transmitter was captured from the Germans in Tunisia and the amplifier came from damaged Italian equipment.

Packed with 300,000 French refugees, underfed, short of fuel and clothing, Algiers at the turn of the year was slowly recovering from the horrors of war. Public dances were prohibited until France was liberated, and in the meantime the hillside city with its towering blocks of hotels and apart-ments took on the role of the 'temporary Paris' of Free French territory.

All restaurants shut down at 8 pm, but servicemen had a choice of fifteen different cinemas then showing films like *The First of the Few*, *Pride and Prejudice* and Walt Disney's *Dumbo*.

When General and Mme de Gaulle attended a charity performance at the Opera House, the ornate façade was brilliantly floodlit and the General walked over a red carpet between lines of white-cloaked African soldiers with drawn swords, the tallest man in the place.

Wearing the plain blue uniform of a chief petty officer, French film actor Jean Gabin arrived at Algiers in a warship; he had once worked on location in the city's Arab quarter, filming his big success *Pepé le Moko*, but threw up a film career in the USA to join the French navy.

Gabin met several old friends again, including Marlene Dietrich, wearing an elegant khaki uniform with USO flashes on the shoulders, and Josephine Baker, in Algiers to recover from a serious operation. Jeep-riding over thousands of miles to entertain troops had hastened an internal com-plaint which caught up with the hard-working revue star in Morocco.

Maisie Griffiths remembered working with her in Egypt: 'I came back to Cairo towards the end of 1943 when Josephine Baker was looking for speciality acts to join her revue for the French troops. I joined the company and on the opening night at some outpost in the desert she asked me to assist her during her act. She wanted me to stand in the wings and pick up her two white fur stoles as she threw them off the stage.

'The first time I caught them I looked back at her and to my surprise she was standing there, poised, with nothing on from the waist up. She told me afterwards that whenever she played to French soldiers, it was not only usual but they always expected it.

'So I saw my first topless show in a dusty camp in the middle of the Sahara Desert.'

Marlene Dietrich gave a show for the services at the Opera House in Algiers and a Press conference for war correspondents in the Aletti Hotel to refute the suggestion that she had joined the USO to lift morale by lifting her skirts. The German-born star told the Press she hoped to give open-air shows to troops in the desert where conditions were primitive, carrying her stage costume and high-heeled shoes in a special carrying-case. She also informed them she had brought forty-eight pairs of nylon stockings with her.

Tommy Trinder, touring North Africa, managed to do fifty shows for the Eighth Army in less than three weeks, as well as several broadcasts in Algiers.

'I was with a small company,' said Trinder, 'and we played Algiers, Cairo and Khartoum and then travelled to Basrah, Jordan, Lebanon and Palestine. From Haifa we went to Cyprus. We also played Jerusalem and I'm probably one of the few Christians who have prayed at the Wailing Wall. We had a refugee there as a driver and I could speak a little Yiddish—having mixed quite impartially with all the London agents—and he told me only Jews could visit the wall, but I went over to it, and beat my chest, and said my piece. To stress my neutrality, I also went into a Moslem mosque.

'A funny thing about our show, five of the artistes in it could all play the piano; Sally Barnes was with me, and Tommy Cooper's wife, Gwen. Once at Lake Timsah as we were relaxing on the beach sunbathing, a troopship passed along the Canal and I heard a soldier shout out my catch-phrase, "You lucky people!" I'm sure he didn't realise I was there.

'Then in Algiers I met a French girl in a show and she spoke a little English; she asked me where I worked in London. The Palladium, I told her. Rubbish, she said, you couldn't work there. You talk too common.

'I dropped in on Algiers on the way home and did some one-man shows – where more than six people constituted an audience – and the Americans asked me to do a show for them. When I said I had to get home to make a film, they promised me a priority flight the next morning. And sure enough, on the flight list there was . . . Viscount Trinder.'

The West End play *Quiet Weekend* was flown out to Algiers with a cast tersely described as nine females and six males; all of them stayed in the ENSA hostel and ate army rations, among them Marjorie Fielding, Frank Cellier, Jan Stuart (later Baroness de Rothschild) and Margaretta Scott who remembers seeing 'the Atlas Mountains covered in snow and oranges growing down below from the roof of the radio station.

'We were playing the Opera House there in February 1944, and by mistake all the scenery went to Cairo with the stage props which meant we had to rehearse in a huge set for *Aida* and paint oranges to look like potatoes. We used a smaller set made from screens for playing in hospitals and I thought it looked ridiculous, until a patient said how good it was to see home through the door; it was very touching.

'In Italy, as a result of some local sabotage, the lights went out during the show and someone had the bright idea of all the audience switching on torches. We played to hundreds of pinpoints of lights.

'It was quite amusing because as soon as a young actress

made an entrance all the torches shone on her, leaving the older members of the company in the dark. Another memory is the flight back from Algiers. As the aircraft taxied along the runway a book fell off the rack and landed on my head. I looked at the title on the cover, it was called *The End of Africa*.'

Georgie Wood met Gracie Fields at Tunis and suggested they do an impromptu show together in Algiers. 'In the Aletti Hotel I saw Al Jolson's pianist, Harry Alst, and it was arranged for Gracie, Jack Benny, Jolson and myself to stage a concert at an air base. Although ENSA didn't allow artistes to appear in USO shows, the ADC in Algiers explained matters to General Eisenhower and it was authorised; it really was a terrific show.

'Before I went overseas for ENSA the maximum pay was £10 a week but I think because of Tommy Trinder we all got £12. When he was told the maximum salary, Tommy said, "Well, I'm sorry, I can't go. I've never worked for less than £12."

'Because of the war I was able to establish to a large extent that the little boy I was playing was not the real me. I remember Sir Oswald Stoll telling me, "You're not a freak, Georgie. You're an individual with a character of your own." And I always disliked the "Wee" prefix in front of my name. Stoll told me I didn't have to rely on my size to make my act acceptable.'

Now in his eighties, Georgie Wood has worked with most of the music-hall greats since the turn of the century. He worked with Charlie Chaplin in Levy and Cardwell's juvenile pantomine company in 1907 – Stan Laurel also worked in the same show before he joined Fred Karno – and on a visit to Hollywood in 1924, he lunched with Chaplin who told him of a day in Oldham when he saw the name 'Wee Georgie Wood' high on all the playbills and wondered if he'd ever see 'Chaplin' in such big letters. He also told him about the day he'd invited some of the chorus-girls from the pantomime to have tea in his digs; Mr Levy, who had parental control over the girls, forbade them to go. Charlie projected his feeling of desolation years later in *The Gold Rush* when he decorated the table with sadly slender resources, tidied the place, brushed his hair, and waited for the girl who never showed up.

ENSA star Judy Shirley worked with Georgie Wood in North Africa; he had known her mother and father well and remembered her as a little girl. After North Africa she was warmly welcomed by the Eighth Army in Italy and chosen as their number one 'Chin-up Girl'; she had worked continuously in the Middle East for eleven months and had already been dubbed 'Queen of the Desert Rats' and 'Number One Gun-site Girl' because of the number of times she had appeared at isolated units.

In 1943 Leslie Henson, rehearsing Shylock in a scene from *The Merchant of Venice* – with Hermione Baddeley as Portia – received a letter from Air Marshal Coningham: 'Do bring a company to see us. I had hoped to promise you a theatre in Rome for Christmas week but it cannot be. Mind you, we can do you very well in Bari or Naples or Foggia and the lads would be thrilled to see you, but do bring a raincoat as it's damned wet. I still have my Italian villa and am saving it for next year. By then I hope to be able to invite you to Paris . . .'

Over 100 ENSA artistes were among the people rescued from a ship which was dive-bombed and then sank in the Mediterranean. Doreen Thompson, one of the girl survivors who was with *Let's Have a Party* company, wrote to her parents at Cockermouth from North Africa describing how it happened:

'We were bombed by a German aircraft and, as we had practised in lifeboat drill, we all went back to our cabins and put on warm clothes. When "emergency stations" sounded we went up to the boat deck and saw the guns blazing at the aircraft with tracer bullets lighting up the sky;

then some RAF aircraft came over and destroyed the German.

'They lowered us into the boats, all the girls first and the troops still on board sang songs to keep our spirits up ... it was a Dutch vessel and the captain had earlier assured us all it was unsinkable. The stewards were all Javanese and they panicked. In fact, scores of them were jumping straight into the water.'

June Lupino and the Mitchell Sisters, Sally and Irene, were in the same lifeboat, and they drifted for some hours before being picked up by an American ship and taken to North Africa.

In London, *Flare Path* finished its run at the Apollo at the end of January 1944 and prepared for a ten-week ENSA tour of the Middle East; *Cradle Song*, directed by John Gielgud went into the Apollo with Yvonne Mitchell in the lead and another Gielgud production, *Crisis in Heaven*, written by Eric Linklater, opened in Edinburgh on 28 February, with Dorothy Dickson and Esmond Knight; *Uncle Harry* was due to open in the West End with Michael Redgrave and Beatrix Lehmann, and a new comedy, Robert Morley's *Staff Dance*, with Morley and Bea Lillie—playing her first straight role in Britain – was on a pre-London tour, and opened at Oxford on 7 February.

A Soldier for Christmas, with Joyce Barbour, Trevor Howard, Robert Beatty and Pauline Letts, succeeded *Quiet Weekend* at Wyndham's, and impresario Bill Linnit hoped that *Quiet Weekend* would resume its record-breaking run after its ENSA tour of the Middle East: it had been presented as a 'command performance' for Queen Mary, the Duke and Duchess of Gloucester, and members of the forces, and ran for two and a half years with 1,059 performances, a record for Wyndham's.

Pauline Letts remembers her West End début. As she reached her big emotional moment in the play a siren sounded close to the theatre: 'For a split second my heart sank and then I determined to put the noise right out of my mind.' The audience was with her. Nobody moved until she finished her speech.

The author of *A Soldier for Christmas*, Reginald Beckwith, was in Italy as a war correspondent for the BBC, and had worked before the war in revue. Beverley Baxter devoted a long column in the *Evening Standard* of 5 February to the play and while he could find nothing but praise for Meriel Forbes's housemaid and Pauline Letts's 'study of marble that melted, to some extent I am sorry that Trevor Howard chose this for his transition from the Arts Theatre. Essentially an actor for Ibsen, Shaw or Shakespeare, he is now doomed to a long run in a part he does well but which could be carried satisfactorily by a less-gifted actor.'

Trevor Howard went to RADA in the mid-thirties, with four other men and twenty girls; 'as he appeared to be the only normal one there at the time he got all the good parts'. He joined the paratroops during the war because he was bored and wanted a bit of drama, but he was terrified, 'especially of the gliding. I did about twenty-two jumps but only one in enemy territory.'

He was invalided out as acting-captain, winning a Military Cross along the way but doesn't want people to know about it: 'I want to forget about the war. All the time I told myself . . . if I came through I was going to make up for lost time.

'Nobody had heard of me and there was absolutely no reason why I should have become a star . . . except they wanted a face that hadn't been seen before for *Brief Encounter*.'

Elsie and Doris Waters, entertaining in military hospitals for over two years, made arrangements to go to India for ENSA in March 1944. For Vera Lynn, who went to India in April 1944, it 'was my first trip to the fighting front'. The Press gave her generous coverage and told their readers how she had earned £50,000 from royalties on her records: '"Yours" alone sold 200,000 copies and Miss Lynn received a halfpenny on each single sold.' More than 600 fans wrote to her most weeks and sometimes as many as 1,000.

A Miss Ruddell of Belfast, in a letter to a newspaper, was obviously not among them. 'Regarding Vera Lynn's salary,' she wrote, 'is £50,000 a large or small sum for a star? How much did she get from ENSA and the BBC? Had she been singing on any of the fronts, and if so, where and for how long?'

Georgie Wood, back from North Africa, topped the bill for Lew Grade in *Tonzafun* in May 1944 at the New Cross Empire, with the Smeddle Brothers and Gracie's brother, Tommy Fields. Georgie went to see Jack Hylton's *Cinderella*, which was enjoying a long run at His Majesty's, with George Moon as Buttons and 'Evelyn Laye, the reason principal boys were invented. And Tessie O'Shea kept on improving just when I thought she was as good as she could be. Of course, as Winchell put it, she was an "Oomph" girl ... every time she sat on a sofa, it went "oomph!" I was due to play Belfast next and remember seeing a Green Room Rag before I left with Naunton Wayne, Eddie Gray and Sid Field as Slasher Green; he had been my understudy in 1917. One of the greatest of all comedians was Sid; he had the two qualities every good performer must have, authority and diffidence. He once told the Friars Club in New York that he had learned his timing from me ...'

Gertrude Lawrence arrived back in London on 18 May after six years in America, looking exactly like the heroine of her last West End play, Noel Coward's *Tonight at 8.30*. She brought with her two small bags, twelve eggs, three packets of butter, an orange and some soap for Mr Coward.

Her first broadcast came from a canteen in Islington when she sang with Geraldo's orchestra, and while waiting for the ban to be lifted so that she could go overseas with ENSA, she visited a concert hall on the south coast and stood on the same stage where she received her first bouquet as a fifteen-year-old unknown.

Ernest Hemingway arrived in the same aircraft as Gertrude

Lawrence and told the waiting newspapermen that he didn't intend to discuss the war, 'I'll leave that to Eisenhower. He knows, I don't. I'm sorry to be so dull, but I'm bad at generalisation. I think any writer – especially a war correspondent – is dull in conversation. It's only the phonies who are personally colourful.'

Some ENSA artistes went so far ahead after D-Day, they
must have done their act in German
Tommy Trinder, 1944

'Before D-Day,' said Donald Sinden, 'the armies began
concentrating around the south coast and we played to many
of them before they went across to Normandy. Security
arrangements meant the blinds were permanently drawn in
the bus, and only our army driver was supposed to know
the destination but, of course, being locals, most of us knew
exactly where we were going every night.'

All leave had been cancelled at the beginning of April 1944
and the invasion troops completely sealed off from the
outside world – they weren't allowed to post letters or to use
the phone boxes. With the possibility of enemy agents
infiltrating coastal resorts, a ban was placed on access to areas
around the coastline from The Wash to the tip of Land's End.

Dora Bryan, the Oldham-born actress was with the
Colchester Repertory Theatre Company at the time and
remembers playing Devizes on the eve of D-Day 'when the
security was terrific. Before we toured the invasion bases we
were warned it was a danger zone, but they assured us we
would be fully protected.'

The Germans sent new bombs across the Channel – pilot-
less rockets designed to destroy London. When the buzzing

stopped, the doodlebug had reached the end of its flight and it fell on whatever was below. The first official note of the arrival of a V-1 rocket on London was on 14 June, when a siren had sounded at 11.37 pm and a report came from Kentish Town station that an explosion had been heard and a dazzling flare seen coming from the direction of Prince of Wales Road. At 11.51 pm signalmen at Farringdon station in the city reported that 'something big had fallen between the station and King's Cross and it sounded like an aircraft'.

During the next three months, 8,000 V-1s were launched against London, with alerts in operation eight and a half hours a day. When they first arrived there were thirty-six West End theatres open; soon only thirteen shows kept going.

Ronald Millar's *Zero Hour*, which ironically enough dealt with the eve of invasion, opened at the Lyric on 14 June, took £9 at the box office the next day and closed on 17 June. Alfred Lunt and Lynn Fontanne, their London season at the Aldwych interrupted by the flying bombs, took *There Shall Be No Night* to Leeds. Gladys Henson remembers *The Druid's Rest* finishing at St Martin's Theatre: 'The doodlebugs started and my charwoman said: "I don't like them half as much as the other bombs, do you?" But it was a shared experience and perhaps it did something for people's dispositions in those days and made them fatalistic. If you were going to get it, you'd get it.'

Richard Burton went into the RAF, and after a short course at Oxford he was posted to a navigator's training school in Canada (with fellow cadet Warren Mitchell). Stanley Baker joined the Birmingham Repertory Company.

'We were living in Gloucester Place,' said Margaretta Scott, 'and I remember John [her husband] hearing what he thought was an aircraft flying over the rooftops and he said: "That chap's very brave, flying so low." And it turned out to be a doodlebug.'

Barbara Mullen was filming at Lime Grove studios in *A Place of One's Own* with Margaret Lockwood, James Mason and Dennis Price when the doodlebugs started coming over: 'We always had to stop working because we were in the top studio. One morning, during a crowd scene, Margaret Lockwood was sitting next to me when the siren sounded. I was full of admiration for her, thinking how brave she was, letting everyone leave the studio first. I was glued to the seat because I was terrified and not able to move.

'Then she turned to me and said: "You really are courageous, staying here like this." I told her I was only sitting there because I couldn't do anything else.

'"Well, neither can I," said Margaret.'

The fiftieth season of the Proms opened at the Albert Hall, but after three weeks the doodlebugs forced the orchestra to conclude the concerts in a BBC studio at Bedford – the third time the war had interrupted the Proms. Sir Henry Wood, in his seventy-fifth year, fell ill at the end of June and died in hospital at Hitchin on 19 August; his ashes were placed in St Sepulchre's church where a stained-glass window was dedicated to his memory in 1946.

Sir Henry's long association with the Promenade concerts began with the opening bars of a Wagner overture on the night of 10 August 1895 (in Austria, Adolf Hitler was six years old), which started a tradition still renewed each year at the Albert Hall when his bronze head is adorned with a laurel wreath on the first night by the Promenaders.

Kate O'Brien's play *The Last of Summer* opened at the Phoenix, and Firth Shephard revived *The Last of Mrs Cheyney* at the Savoy with Coral Browne as Mrs Cheyney and Jack Buchanan playing Lord Dilling, supported by Athene Seyler, James Dale and Fanny Rowe.

The play defied the doodlebugs and was taking over £2,500 a week at the box office.

The Old Vic company with Dame Sybil Thorndike, Laurence Olivier and Ralph Richardson at the helm, sailed confidently into rehearsals for the first three plays of the season: *Richard III*, *Peer Gynt* and *Arms and the Man*. The company included Nicholas Hannen, Arnold Ridley and a newcomer to the West End 'of whom much was expected', Margaret Leighton who had been playing leading parts at the Birmingham Repertory Theatre.

George Black had a revue in preparation for the Palladium entitled *If It's Laughter You're After*, starring Tommy Trinder, Zoe Gail, Jewel and Warris and Elisabeth Welch – some months back from doing an ENSA revue at Gibraltar with Bea Lillie, Edith Evans, Jeanne de Casalis, John Gielgud and Michael Wilding. And Ivor Novello was writing a new musical called *Perchance to Dream* . . .

By the end of June ENSA was making preparations to send concert parties and plays over to Normandy – George Formby and Leslie Henson were among the first to volunteer, supported by Gertrude Lawrence, Alice Delysia and the pianist, Solomon.

Twenty-seven officers and 180 other ranks were detailed to cover the entertainment front in Western Europe, and the first diversions for front-line troops were music broadcasts from loudspeaker vans of everything from Handel's *Messiah* to a new song written after the invasion (by Michael Carr and Tommy Connor) called 'All's Well, Mademoiselle'.

By July, as well as advance film units with their own generators and standard cinema projectors, there were over a hundred ENSA soubrettes waiting to cross to France, and on 13 July 'Column One' was ready with *Variety Calls* and George Formby's unit. Four more companies comprised 'Column Two': *We Six*; *Here's How*; *All Swell* and *We're Here*. Apart from Formby's company the contingent was divided into three mobile columns, each consisting of two parties of six with their own transport, sleeping accommodation, portable stage and lighting equipment.

Donald Sinden remembers his company being asked to take a play to France: '[Charles F.] Smith received a polite request from ENSA, "Could we take you under our wing for the European tour?" This was fine for the actors because it meant our salaries immediately went up to £10 a week. We took *Normandy Story* into France, Belgium and, eventually into Germany. We were playing in Schleswig-Holstein when the European war finished and as the Japanese war was still on, it was decided to send us out to India and we toured the South-East Asia Command from Calcutta as far as Burma.'

After D-Day Terry-Thomas took a *Stars in Battledress* show to Europe: 'We travelled through France and Belgium as they were liberated, and got to Germany in May 1945. By then I was wearing a wonderful uniform with a smart fur collar specially made for me by a talented tailor in Brussels who as well as being an art connoisseur was also a personal friend of Winston Churchill. You know even as a young man working in Smithfield Market I was always very conscious about my appearance.

'I always wore suede shoes and carried a small malacca cane. The porters used to refer to me as "that comical spark with the stick and the brown velvet slippers".

'Back in London to be demobbed I was anxious to get out as soon as I could. I'd told thousands of troops all over Europe that they'd see me in a West End show after the war and I wanted to keep my promise. A chap in Army Welfare suggested that I should ask for a month's compassionate leave and then keep on renewing the request every few weeks – advice I thankfully followed. It meant I was able to draw army pay while scouting around looking for work. I managed to go straight into *Piccadilly Hayride* with Sid Field at the Prince of Wales, and did my "Technical Hitch" and it stole most of the notices.

'It eventually earned me at least £100,000. Mind you, sometimes I sit at home in Ibiza and wonder if I shouldn't have been more ambitious. I don't mean more *inventive*, but at the beginning I was doing a lot of writing and perhaps I should have developed that more instead of giving the public what it wanted. One thing that puzzles me is where on earth have the last twenty years gone? The time seems to have gone past so terribly quickly, mainly, I suppose, because I've never stopped working. Never mind, I've enjoyed it all.'

On 12 August a notice was pinned on a leave camp's information board: 'Today at 14.30 and 17.00 hours there will be an ENSA show . . . with George Formby.' The leave camp, an orchard concealed in a Normandy valley, was a centre for soldiers who had been in the front line a long time.

Thousands of them, back for a day's rest, watched the ENSA convoy arrive, led by a despatch rider on his motorbike, and the artistes following in a bus with the star sitting in front with the driver. Then came the stage truck and finally the escorting officer in his jeep. The convoy moved slowly up an avenue signposted 'Piccadilly', passing the 'Café Royal' and 'The Polytechnic' – a rest room where papers and magazines were issued (or rather a plain marquee as were all the other London-named landmarks) to stop at a clearing known as 'Regent's Park', a natural amphitheatre where the portable stage was put up.

As fighter aircraft spiralled across a hazy blue sky, volunteers helped to lay out benches and set the stage, hoisting a mini-piano over the footlights. There was applause for the musical introduction by pianist Ivan Fosello (a Mantovani musician until he became an ARP warden in 1940) and the singing of a tall blonde from Devon, Pauline Forrest, who gave them operatic airs. For an encore Miss Forrest sang a particularly beautiful *Carmen*.

Next on the bill was Alexandria, a versatile accordionist who finished her act with a leggy display of acrobatic dancing that soon had the boys sitting up straighter on the benches and a brisk trade going at the back for the loan of a pair of service binoculars. Alexandria knew her stuff: Miss Drina Ogden had been doing it for two years, first with the Canadian Legion and later for ENSA. It was only because George Formby was on next that the troops let her finish at all.

There was a full-throated roar for George and his little ukelele as he sang the songs they all knew, from 'Leaning on a Lamp-post' to 'It Serves You Right, You Joined', and then gave them a new one 'Rolling into France'. There was time between shows for a few sandwiches, cakes and a cup of tea and then a fresh audience filled the arena. George finished the eighth encore and then it was time to go. The company had another date to play that evening, fifteen kilometres away across some very uncertain roads.

Did George Formby or any of the other ENSA artistes in Normandy know that 'Vaudeville' had been born there? Many years before François Villon sang his songs and recited his poems in the wine shops of Paris, a gentleman called Olivier Basselin was praising Normandy cider in popular song; he owned a fulling mill in the valley of Vaux de Vire from which his lyrics took their name, later corrupted to 'Vaudeville'.

Ben Lyon flew Bebe Daniels to Omaha Beach and she was able to make some recordings with the American wounded to demonstrate the speed and efficiency with which they could be flown out of Normandy to a service hospital at Oxford the same day. She was later decorated with the Medal of Freedom, the highest US civilian award, by order of President Roosevelt. She also did recorded interviews with medical specialists for the US Mutual Radio network.

'It was difficult', said Ben, 'because great care had to be taken to check that the wounded men were still alive when the programmes were broadcast. This was long before tapes and they were all done on discs with, as far as I can remember, Alister Scott-Johnson as producer. Before I left London the last time they played one of the recordings on a BBC radio show, and you could still hear the sound of guns firing in Normandy.

'I remember we received a letter right at the start of the war telling us the American Embassy couldn't guarantee our protection if we stayed in England, and Bebe said to Val Parnell: "We're not going anywhere. Britain's been wonderful to us and we're not going to run out on her just when she's in trouble", so we stayed.'

A Soldier for Christmas was one of the first plays in

Europe. Trevor Howard wasn't with the company, he had stayed in London to start filming *The Way to the Stars*.

'We played Rouen and Dieppe,' recalled Pauline Letts, 'and in Dieppe there was no heating so we spent most of our free time huddled over tiny little oil lamps, shivering. One night there were 4,000 GIs in the audience and an American orchestra in the pit; when the show was over they played the "Marseillaise", the "Stars and Stripes" and "God Save the King" in that order, which I thought showed great tact. In Holland we played Eindhoven and Tilberg.

'There was no electricity at Tilberg so we made up by candlelight, with a large hole in the roof and a crescent moon shining down on the dressing-room.

'The front line was only twenty-six miles away, and the troops came back from the fighting each night just to see the play and I think they all enjoyed it. In the streets during the day the Dutch children spat at us, possibly they mistook us for Germans in our ENSA uniforms.'

Diana Wynyard, Margaret Rutherford and Ivor Novello landed in Normandy on 19 August and gave their first performance of *Love from a Stranger* within the sound of gunfire. This was shortly after Novello had been released from prison after serving three months for a petrol-coupon offence. While in France he composed a song for his new show and introduced 'We'll Gather Lilacs' to the troops in a Bayeux theatre before it was published in London.

Basil Dean, in Normandy to see the play, remembers coming across Florence Desmond and Kay Cavendish there 'when they demanded battledress and gumboots from me after flatly turning down all suggestions at Drury Lane that they should wear ENSA uniforms'. He noticed other exotic versions of regimentals like the shark-skin tropical outfit of musical-comedy star (and friend of King Farouk) Constance Carpenter, and writer Naomi Jacob's khaki tunic of antique cut with claret-coloured facings and brightly polished captain's pips on the shoulders, 'the uniform of a woman's organisation in World War I'. She was welfare supervisor in Italy. And Gertrude Lawrence was ready for the Second Front in an American Red Cross uniform 'with ENSA shoulder flashes, a USO badge on the pocket and a steel helmet to complete the martial effect.'

Florence Desmond was on a three-week tour with Kay Cavendish and Flanagan and Allen, and as the two women wore civilian clothes they were continually being stopped along the way and questioned. Numbers of collaborators were mingling with refugees and trying to escape.

They were issued with ENSA battledresses in Bayeux and Bud Flanagan took one look at them and said: 'Oh, gorblimey, look at those two, Lanky and Shorthouse!' Miss Desmond took up her needle and did some instant home tailoring. When a GI asked her what the ENSA badges stood for, she explained it meant 'Every Night Something 'Appens'.

'I went over again in June 1945,' said Florence Desmond, 'and worked in Germany. One night a car came to collect me to do a show for officers and their friends. "What about the troops?" I asked.

'"We're afraid there's no room for the soldiers in the theatre," they said.

'"No room for the men?" I shouted at them. "I haven't come all this way just to entertain a shower of officers. You'd better all move back and make room for them on the floor." And they did as I suggested.

'We had a narrow escape on the first visit with Bud and Chesney Allen. I think it was north of Amiens where we were ambushed by German snipers who had felled some trees and blocked the road. Fortunately for us there were some Free French guerrillas close by and they chased the Germans into a nearby forest.'

Gertrude Lawrence and her party were marooned for five hours on a motor raft on the river Seine. Their small convoy had been cruising along crater-torn roads strewn with wrecked German vehicles and dead soldiers until they came to the bank of the river where a squad of Canadian engineers put them aboard the raft to cross over. Setting out at 7 pm, the motor stopped and they were carried downstream. DUKWs (amphibious vehicles used for waterborne troop operations) tried to tow them in but found it impossible in a strong cross breeze. When the raft eventually started to sink, the party had to take to the escorting DUKW. They lost most of their possessions and spent a cold night in a nearby château.

Richard Hearne ('Mr Pastry') remembers playing a town in Normandy called La Deliverance: 'We were billeted on the top floor of a house three storeys high and on the first night there, a German gun at Le Havre was firing towards Bayeux and the shells seemed to whistle right past the windows.

'Going through the Falaise Gap we did a show at Villiers-Boccageand when we arrived the place had been bulldozed flat so we had to entertain the troops in a field. Halfway through an officer walked down between the rows of soldiers calling out different men's names; as he called out each one, the man stood up and left.

'Apparently Monty was just across the hedge, handing out decorations. We were terribly disappointed he didn't stop to see the show.'

Hearne toured many of the towns in Europe he had visited as a small boy with his circus father and was with the first ENSA party into Antwerp, where he stood on the roof of the Sports Palace and watched the army dealing with snipers in the suburbs.

'And on the way towards Paris we slept anywhere, any house that still had a roof; one night we even had to sleep on a dining-room table. The troops seemed to move so quickly we almost got left but we did manage to be in Brussels for the liberation. As all our army lorries drove slowly through the town, the women held up their babies to have their little hands shaken by the soldiers. It was a wonderful thing to see . . . and a thrilling place to be in at the time, especially when our driver was caught in crossfire.

'I was possibly the first British civilian to enter Hertogen-bosch after it was liberated. I'd gone forward to see if it was OK to do the show and halfway along the road we ran into a German resistance pocket and shells whizzed over my head. It didn't seem practical to turn back so we pressed on and as we approached two blown-up tanks, an officer came running towards us to warn us that the road was mined. Then we had to turn back. We made it next day and fortunately the theatre was still in good shape.'

In Paris, on 26 August, de Gaulle and General Jacques Philippe Leclerc (later killed in an air crash in Algeria) marched under the Arc de Triomphe to place some flowers on the Tomb of the Unknown Soldier. The flame on the tomb had remained burning throughout the German occupation. Then de Gaulle faced the cheering crowds in the Place d'Etoile (now the Place de Gaulle) and reminded them that they were in Paris, the city by the Seine, 'which stood erect and rose in order to free herself – Paris oppressed, downtrodden and martyred [for the second time in her history: German soldiers had also marched through her streets in 1817] but still Paris. Free now, freed by the hands of Frenchmen, the capital of fighting France, the great and eternal.'

And as he spoke, the crowds cheered amidst a blanket of artillery fire from German guns outside the city, and as they joined the generals in the march along the Champs Elysées more firing broke out and spread all over the city. It was later thought to be a prearranged last stand by collaborators and fifth columnists who, unlike the Germans, could not surrender.

Once the cheering stopped, the city air became more menacing. Parisians were full of fears; fear of starving, of ill-health, and mostly of informers. Women were stripped of their furs in the street by patriots as a gesture against profiteers and collaborators. Sixty per cent of the people were underfed, badly clothed and suffering from anaemia with thousands of them eating nothing but dried beans or boiled potatoes. Those with money were able to buy black-market meat, and eggs sold at 25 francs each.

Yet the theatres were doing good business, and the Opera sold out half an hour after the box office opened. Fashion experts, including 'Coco' Chanel, were able to stage four shows a year. After the liberation, the legendary fashion and perfume leader, Gabrielle Chanel had been arrested by the Resistance Movement, but she was held for less than three hours and despite her association with high-ranking Nazi officers, she was later cleared of collaboration charges.

Maurice Chevalier, who died aged eighty-three in January 1972, stayed in France throughout the occupation and was also alleged to have collaborated with the Germans and subsequently banned from entering Britain and the USA. Later, when wartime memories had faded he made triumphant comebacks in both countries.

The little sparrow, singer Edith Piaf, continued to give concerts during 1940–4 and sang for French prisoners-of-war, and is believed to have acted as a messenger for the Resistance, carrying false identities to enable some of the prisoners to escape from the camps. Paris-born Charles Aznavour, who was nineteen when the Allies liberated Paris, had grown up in a restaurant run by his parents, an actor and a singer.

The restaurant closed down in 1939 when his father joined the army, and Charles was forced to sell papers on the streets for a living until he managed to get a job as an actor with a touring company. There followed the inevitable years of failure and rejection until he began to write songs; he first tasted success when he went into partnership with Pierre Roche, and stars like Mistinguett, Chevalier and Piaf asked them to write their songs.

The writer Gertrude Stein was discovered by a *Life* magazine photographer at Culoz in south-eastern France where she was living with a companion-secretary and a poodle, and hoping for news of her latest book, *All Wars Are Interesting*, which was to be published in America by

Random House. In a joyful mood on her day of liberation, the seventy-year old Miss Stein called it, 'the day of days and what a day it is today; that is, what a day it was the day before yesterday'.

Poet John Pudney, then in the RAF, met up with Pablo Picasso who had endured privation under the Nazis: 'He showed me German magazines and collaborationist newspapers in which his work had been attacked and where he was described as "Picasso the Jew . . . the decadent Pablo, the obscene pornographer". People were soon queueing to view his wartime paintings, all stored in the upper rooms of his Paris house.'

On D-Day plus seventeen the RAF Gang Show's Number One Unit landed in France. 'We followed the army as they advanced,' said Dick Emery, 'all the way through France and Holland and as far as my own work was concerned it was marvellous training.

'It was then, travelling around in the back of a three-ton lorry – sometimes doing over 240 miles in a single day – that I began to develop some of the characters like the blonde Mandy.'

Cardew Robinson remembers travelling in the lorry through France to do a show and 'we must have gone the wrong way; we ended up about half a mile from the German lines.

'Our driver, who was a local civilian, drove slowly past a sentry who called out, "Hey you! Where the effing hell do you think *you're* going?"

'All my memories of wartime *Gang Shows* feature outraged NCOs yelling, "Where the effing hell are *you* going?" I told him with a certain theatrical dignity that "We were on our way to do a show".

'"Oh yes?" he sneered, "Who to, the effing Germans? If you keep going, you can't miss them." He hadn't finished talking before the lorry turned a complete half-circle . . .

'I would say it was a great help to me to work in the *Gang Shows* in those days. If nothing else, it meant I was lucky enough to be able to do my own job as an entertainer with chaps who were either professionals from pre-war shows or ex-scouts who had worked in the civilian *Gang Shows*.'

In September Emlyn Williams headed an ENSA company that toured France, Belgium and Holland, and included Ambrosine Phillpotts, Jacqueline Clarke and Jessie Evans.

Ambrosine Phillpotts recalled: 'The play was *Blithe Spirit* and we were the next company after Diana Wynyard and Ivor Novello to play Caen. Emlyn wanted us to go on to Nijmegen after Eindhoven, but the ENSA people in charge made a fuss, saying it was too near the front line. Emlyn told them that's where we should be, but Montgomery turned up and he said it was too soon for a show: there were still German snipers in the neighbourhood.

'The most memorable thing about the tour was that for the first time in my life I was playing to an audience composed entirely of men; it was their laughter that stuck in my mind. Normally there's a mixture of men and women in the theatre . . . but to hear thousands of men laughing; I've never heard such a marvellous sound. Unless you've acted in front of soldiers, you've never heard a sound quite like it.'

The caretaker at the Trianon Theatre at Caen was eighteen-year-old 'Madeleine X' who carried a photograph of an RAF airman she came across in 1943 after he had been shot down in Normandy. She nursed him secretly, but when he recovered and left she was betrayed and put in prison; after serving a sentence she was forced to hide in a wood to avoid being sent to a labour camp by the Nazis.

In October, Gertrude Lawrence opened a season at the Scala Theatre in Antwerp and *Love from a Stranger* was playing Brussels. An ENSA variety company was three miles from the German frontier at Nijmegen when their truck was shelled and all their props and musical instruments were destroyed. The company manager, Jack Dagmar, hastily wrote some new sketches to fit in with the situation. A soldier sent a letter home to the local paper relating how he was stationed 'in a big town in Belgium, still held on its northern outskirts by the Germans. We were careful not to antagonise the enemy the night of an ENSA concert. We wanted to enjoy the show and the electricity supply which provided the current for the footlights was still in their section.'

Solomon the pianist made the first live broadcast to people of both occupied and liberated Holland from *Herrijzend Nederland* ('The Rising Netherlands') the only radio station on Free Dutch soil. It had been secretly built by the Dutch underground during the war and began operating at the end of September 1944.

Bessie Marsh, in charge of the ENSA hostel in Brussels in October, had spent over two years in a concentration camp. In Belgium as a child she was caught fleeing over the frontier in 1940 and placed in a camp with hundreds of other women aged from sixteen to seventy. 'We were treated reasonably well,' she said, 'until the Allied advance into Europe and then things got very bad.'

Early in November 1944, members of the Nervo and Knox ENSA revue narrowly escaped death when anti-personnel bombs were dropped near them by the Germans. One fell within 20 yd of the theatre, another 15 yd away while Nelson Holt was doing his mind-reading act onstage with his partner Kusharney; although injured by shell splinters, they continued with the act. Pianist Nellie Boyd-Taylor was hit on the back of the neck by shrapnel, and many of the girls' costumes were slashed by flying glass and fragments of bombs as they hung in the dressing room . . . but the show went on.

North of Nijmegen a Sergeant Newing parked his mobile gramophone unit to play records for the front-line soldiers.

'Turn it loud, sarge,' suggested one of the soldiers, 'and let the Jerries hear it as well.'

The sergeant turned the volume full on and the melodious strains of Bing Crosby singing 'Yodel Boy' boomed through the speakers towards the German lines.

They immediately reciprocated by firing a shell which carried away three loudspeakers and half the sergeant's van.

'Sorry sarge,' said the soldier, 'but isn't that just like them? No sense of humour.'

It was planned to transmit broadcasts of ENSA shows to troops back to the United Kingdom, and with the BBC and Radio Nationale Belgique ENSA set up its own recording outfit with a van touring the forward areas to record the difficult conditions in which the companies performed.

In Paris, ENSA's new 'Capital Cities Service' opened with all-star productions then being staged in the Marigny Theatre. The first production was *Gay Salute* starring, appropriately enough, Noel Coward and others were *A Soldier for Christmas* and *Lady from Edinburgh*, with Dulcie Gray.

The first entertainment for Allied troops in Paris had been staged at the Marigny Theatre on 16 November, with Noel Coward, Frances Day, Bobby Howes, Nervo and Knox and Geraldo and his orchestra. Among the audience was the British Ambassador and Lady Diana Duff Cooper, and Mrs Anthony Eden.

Shaw's *Arms and the Man*, with Richard Greene and his wife Patricia Medina (later Mrs Joseph Cotten), was presented to troops a mile from the Germans in a forward area on 20 November, and all along the front lines of the Allied advance, tens of thousands of vehicles and mobile guns massed, with Red Cross trucks and ammunition lorries continually moving forward. A little way behind them, ENSA chorus-girls in flimsy costumes danced in front of tin-hatted infantrymen just out of the slit-trenches. Overhead, fighter aircraft circled backwards and forwards, keeping a watchful eye on the enemy . . . and the sounds heard were the noise of battle: the deep rumble thunder of Allied artillery pounding the Germans at the least sign of movement.

Theatre designer Rex Whistler – who had done the costumes and scenery for *An Ideal Husband* in 1943, and for Sadler's Wells *Le Spectre de la Rose* in 1944 – was killed near the village of Mesnil, near Caen, during his first hours of action. A tank troop leader leading an attack across the river Orne, he was caught by a shellburst.

Whistler, who had been commissioned in the Welsh Guards in the winter of 1939, still kept up his designing until he was posted to Arromanches in Normandy with the Guards Armoured Division at the end of June 1944. Thirty-nine when he died, he left a mural on the walls of the officers' mess at Brighton which was transferred to Brighton Art Gallery after the war.

There was serious rioting towards the end of November in Brussels, with four civilians killed and thirty injured. Many gendarmes were also injured in clashes with demonstrators shouting: 'Down with Pierlot!' He was the Belgian Prime Minister whose policies were under attack. ENSA's Garrison Theatre (formerly the Théâtre Royal du Parc), with Sergeant-Major Cyril Berlin in charge backstage, became a casualty station while the riot lasted.

Once peace was restored to the city, Army Welfare requisitioned several hotels so that leave troops could enjoy a brief freedom from the front line (then 60 miles away), with breakfast in bed and entertainment in the evening, all on the army.

Run in conjunction with ENSA and Naafi, there was an information bureau, welfare centre and gift shop. The hotels employed 500 girls to look after the soldiers; they also went out at night in parties of fifty to attend forces dances.

Brussels by then was the brightest and most crowded city in liberated Europe. The Avenue Louise was still one of the most elegant and sophisticated shopping streets on the Continent, and the troops could walk along the Grand Place to look at the tall eighteenth-century mansions or explore the forest of Soignes and walk over an autumnal carpet of multi-coloured beech leaves on Wellington's road to Waterloo. Or there were the open-air markets along the cobbled Sablon section, and the wide boulevards skirting peaceful lakes dotted with white swans; the towering

Cinquantenaire Arch lending a Parisian air to the city. Cognac and champagne were available in plentiful supply in the Rue des Dominicians, two hours from the combat zone. But there was a snag: army pay was still so poor the soldiers couldn't afford the prices.

In Antwerp, Belgium's second city, there was the cathedral to see and the splendid Renaissance town hall, a pleasant stroll from the station down the Keyserlei and Meir towards the river Scheldt, and the waterfront promenade near the Old Steen fortress.

The troops were able to walk through the zoological gardens to see the spectacle of Belgian collaborators housed where the lions and the monkeys used to be – men and women, some awaiting trial and others condemned to death standing or lying on straw behind the bars of the cages with a few rough blankets for bedclothes.

Back in London a postcard, written earlier in the year from a prison camp in Germany, arrived at the Cumberland Hotel, Marble Arch. The message was: 'Please reserve two rooms with bath for two Royal Canadian Air Force officers for the week beginning 15 October 1944. Also please book four good seats for one of the popular shows now running and put them on the bill.' The sender, a flying-officer, added that he would be grateful for a confirmation of the bookings. The management replied by return, reserving the accommodation and booking the seats. There was one extra detail: the whole thing was on the house.

A travelling repertory season was inaugurated in Birmingham parks in the summer of 1944, with Yvonne Mitchell and Hester Paton Browne starring in *Pygmalion*, *The Constant Wife*, and *Tonight at 8.30*. ENSA shows touring in Britain included *The Quaker Girl*, with Celia Lipton and Billy Milton (out of the RAF); *The Love Racket*, with Carol Raye and Arthur Askey, and *The Lilac Domino*, with Graham Payne, long-time companion of Noel Coward, and Leo

Franklyn. John Mills and his wife Mary Hayley Bell were in *All Adrift* with Bernard Miles touring the Orkneys, and actors from the Polish Air Force toured the play *Husband by Courtesy*, starring Polish singer Helena Makowska who had managed to escape from a German concentration camp.

Lionel Blair was 'playing child parts at Stratford-upon-Avon with people like Helen Cherry and Andrew Faulds' (Faulds is now a Socialist Member of Parliament).

Joyce, Blair's sister, moved to Oxford with her mother when the doodlebugs started falling, and she attended school in Chipping Norton.

'During the war we were never really parted from the family and quite honestly, in spite of the bombs and everything, I remember those days as happy ones. I went to the Cone-Ripman Drama School in Upper Grosvenor Street, travelling from Stamford Hill every day and occasionally in the afternoons we'd play baseball in Hyde Park with some GIs. I had a good friend at the school – she's still a friend today – and that was Joan Collins.

'Julie Andrews was there at the same time and I remember her asking me whether I lived far away. In carefully modulated tones she said : "If it's not too far from me, perhaps you would care to come to my house for tea. I'll ask mummy to make a chocolate cake specially for you."'

Lionel returned to London after his Shakespeare season : 'I went into a play with Phyllis Dare and Albert Chevalier called *June Mad* – directed by John Fernald – and through it I was up for an audition for a part in *Kiss and Tell*. Roger Moore, who was a student at RADA at the time, auditioned for the same part, but I was lucky enough to get it and we opened at the Phoenix Theatre.'

Meanwhile, on the overseas front again, Joyce Grenfell flew out to Iraq to give a series of concerts for the wounded in hospitals, and at her first performance was introduced by a nervous but enthusiastic entertainments officer who told the men: 'And now I'm delighted to say that this wonderful lady has travelled all the way to Baghdad...just to entertain you all in bed.'

Faith Brook set off for Italy in 1944 in a party of twelve men and three women: 'It was a case of *Stars in Battledress* going out of the blackout into the sunlight...I think we were lucky to see Italy at that time with a war on, although I don't think I heard anything louder than the backfire of a truck the whole eight months we were there. There were the usual frustrations: we were army but ENSA was responsible for the routing and if anything went wrong neither Army Welfare nor ENSA wanted to know. For instance my kitbag was pinched from the back of the lorry between Naples and Rome and I was left with nothing but the clothes I was wearing at the time. I told the army who referred me to ENSA and after days of going from one to the other I got fed up and appealed to the Americans. I spent the next six months walking about in a pair of GI pants with a GI shirt to match.

'There seemed to be a strange lack of communication all round; whenever we arrived somewhere they either expected us the week previously or they didn't expect us until the week after. We went from Naples to Bari on one trip and it turned into a nightmare and nearly proved disastrous for me.

'We were the only entertainment unit in a convoy of military personnel – about twenty lorries in all – and we got stuck in the snow somewhere near Foggia. Eventually we were forced to turn back and finally arrived at ENSA headquarters to report to Lieutenant-Colonel Nigel Patrick. Our sergeant had gone ahead of us as we trooped, tired, cold and starving up the stairs and there was Colonel Patrick waiting for us outside the door of his apartment. In his hand, a noble glass of brandy, in the background a lovely log fire.

'He studied us impersonally for a moment or two and then he said, "Oh, you're back."

'I exploded. "Yes, we're back! We've been thirteen hours on the bloody lorry...no food...freezing cold...and the fucking chains didn't fit the fucking tyres..." I stopped to draw breath.

'"Sergeant," said Patrick crisply, "put Private Brook on a charge...insubordination to a superior officer."

'It was a highly charged dramatic moment and the theatrical element in all of us relished it.

'In the end, Nigel Patrick relented and nothing more was said. We eventually got to Bari...by train.

'We realised by this time the idea of doing a repertoire of plays wouldn't work. It was a very different situation from playing in England; in Italy the army was on the move the whole time so all we had to do was stay put and do one play, and we'd have a different audience each night. We did this in Bari for a month and then went to Taranto for another four weeks and finally we were posted to Athens.

'The month in Athens was the best time of all from my point of view. Apart from loving the city, Hugh Hunt and William Devlin were both there and they looked after us. Not only were we able to present our whole repertoire, but we had the beautiful National Theatre to work in and simply being in one good theatre for a whole month—and playing something other than *Someone at the Door*—was a treat in itself. Afterwards it was back to Italy and playing tiny places along the coast as far north as Rimini.'

Harry Secombe's battalion had been posted to North Africa in 1942—his division was the first to arrive in Tunis—and while there he took part in a show staged at the Metaxas Theatre, doing impersonations of officers and a few blackout sketches.

'After we'd invaded Sicily in 1943 a few of us, all amateurs, formed our own concert party, *The Sicily-Billies*, and we used to perform on the back of a truck: the usual collection of bits and pieces. We were on the move the whole time so we had to make our own entertainment. We worked hard with the show whenever we came out of action, but as soon as the invasion of Italy began in September 1943 we were back in battle again. By the time the North African campaign was over we had captured an entire military band – all German musicians – and they used to play for us at Carthage behind a roped enclosure while we all swam and sunbathed and lolled around on the beach.

'In Italy we were playing a convalescent camp in mid-winter and I was caught in a blizzard and ended up with frostbite and exposure. They sent me to a transit hospital to thaw out and then I found myself in a rest camp where the concert party badly needed some new performers. I was very pleased to join them because by then I'd had more than enough of battles raging loud and long. And it meant being able to play on proper stages for the first time so I grabbed at it.

'We put on a show for the Americans at Bari where I remember discovering Carroll Levis, of all people, in the audience, and I also met some of the GIs' *This is the Army* company; one of them was Joe Allen Probat, who was the original voice for Disney's Donald Duck.

'Fortunately I was able to continue as an entertainer even when I was posted back to an artillery depot. I remember we were all under canvas shortly before Christmas 1944 and naturally it was pouring with rain the whole time, but we were so busy preparing a new show, it didn't bother us very much. In this party we even had our own band; one of the instrumentalists was Bill Hall [who started his Bill Hall Trio not long afterwards with Spike Milligan and another musician].

'This show, produced by Captain John Langston, had everything: lights, dimmers, curtains, costumes and all the props we needed . . . it was the start of a permanent army entertainment unit called *The RATD Follies* and I worked out my shaving routine – based on the way other people shaved – when we needed some new comedy. I discovered that army audiences never cared for blue material, which was fine for me because I never used it anyway; and it was about this time I began to think in terms of turning professional when the war ended.

'Andy Gray of the *Union Jack* army newspaper saw one of our shows and he gave me a great write-up. When I told him I was thinking of going into the business full-time, he suggested I should write to the Windmill Theatre and ask for an audition . . . as a matter of fact he was the first chap to help me get started after the war.

'When the whole think looked like finishing and the troop shows finally began to break up, I was attached to the Central Pool of Artists – *Stars in Battledress* – and stationed just outside Naples.

'The Commanding Officer was Philip Slessor but the only time he ever spoke to me personally in those days was when he saw me strolling casually through the town in a brightly coloured scarf which I felt perfectly matched my suede desert boots. All he said was, "Get that damned scarf off, Lance-Bombardier, you're improperly dressed!" The next time we met was when I was doing a *Variety Bandbox* broadcast and he was a BBC announcer, and of course we greeted each other like a couple of old wartime comrades.

'Naples seemed to be packed with entertainers towards the end of the war; Spike Milligan had joined up with Bill Hall, and Norman Vaughan had joined us – I believe Norman had been in the business just before the war as a "Steffani Silver Songster" – and I remember meeting Nigel Patrick and people like Hector Ross and Ken Platt. I was made principal comic and we toured a full orchestra, with Spike coming on as a singing gypsy. He wanted to play it straight which wasn't easy for him, particularly as he had to wear a pair of brown plimsolls dyed black to match his dress suit that had been converted from a pair of old blackout curtains. I stayed with the show until it was time for demob and a triumphant return to Swansea.

'I kept in touch with Andy Gray and also Isidore Green [who had worked on the *Union Jack*], and they advised me to try my luck in London. Jimmy Grafton was my first agent and I'm still with him . . . and I met Jimmy Edwards and Michael Bentine. In fact I introduced Michael to Spike, and possibly as a result of that meeting the Goons were born.

'The great thing for me about starting in show business at the end of the war was that I'd already experienced so much. I'd cut the ties with home as soon as I joined the army and I'd been shouted at, shot at, and shelled from a great height . . . nothing had much significance after that, not for a very long time. Even a Windmill audience couldn't scare me after being in the Royal Artillery for so long.'

Emlyn Williams was in Italy in 1944, having toured the Middle East with a company that included Kathleen Harrison. She remembers seeing Carroll Levis in Cairo and recalls his advice to the company: 'You must all buy some camel-hide trunks while you're out here; they'll last a lifetime.'

'So we all ordered three pairs each, in different sizes,' said Kathleen, 'and they were delivered a few days before we left. While we were packing, someone accidently knocked a corner on one of my trunks and I discovered layers of brown paper underneath – they were completely fake.

'I remember when we walked along the main streets, the anti-British feeling was beginning among the local Egyptians and they even spat at us in the Muski. We stayed at the Savoy-Continental Hotel in Opera Square and did the plays across the road in the Opera House, three times a day with troops coming in from the Western Desert to see them. We did *Blithe Spirit* which they all appeared to enjoy; and *Night Must Fall* and *Flare Path*, neither of them too popular with war-weary soldiers.

'I loved staying at the Summer Palace Hotel at Alexandria. From there we used to go out into the desert and play to camps within a 200 mile radius. We went as far as Mersa Matruh and I would have loved to have swam in the beautiful lagoon there, but they had only just finished clearing it; it had been full of the dead bodies of German soldiers.

'We went on to Naples on a Dutch boat and stopped in Capua where there were only two places left untouched by the bombing, a brothel and a lunatic asylum. The Americans who were billeted in the brothel were told to leave and they somehow got the idea a new 'Madam' was moving in with her girls and all the GIs lined up in readiness. In fact they even followed us into taxis and up to our rooms at first and made a general nuisance of themselves until it was sorted out and the commanding officer explained that our particular entertainment was on somewhat different lines...

'Otherwise, it was quite a pleasant place, that brothel. There was one very big salon where all the men slept; Jessie Evans shared one bedroom with me and Lueen McGrath had another one with magnificent paintings on the ceiling. But there was no hygiene at all; the lavatory was simply a grille let into the marble floor and there were no baths so we used to stand up and have a wash down in a basin.'

Flare Path had been produced in Cairo immediately following its London run, and Emlyn Williams recalled how Flight-Lieutenant Terence Rattigan had also written another West End hit of 1944, *While the Sun Shines*.

Rattigan, an air-gunner in 1944, had written *Flare Path* while stationed in West Africa. He was returning home when the aircraft began to lose height and the order came to throw everything overboard; he was about to jettison a small case when he remembered it contained the only manuscript of *Flare Path* – written in pencil in an old exercise book. Tearing off the cardboard covers to make the precious script as light as possible he managed to hang on to the loose sheets.

Churchill saw the play in London and said to Adrienne Allen (who was in *Flare Path*) after the show: 'I was very moved by this play. It is a masterpiece of understatement.' He paused and then added, 'But we're rather good at that, aren't we?'

Sir Terence Rattigan attended the Haymarket Theatre in 1972 when an audience of theatrical stars applauded his forty years contribution to the profession and the knighthood he had received earlier that same year. His first big success, *French Without Tears,* opened at the Criterion Theatre in 1936 and continued for 1,039 performances, earning him £23,000.

In 1944 he wrote the script of *The Way to the Stars*, still regarded as one of the finest British wartime films, about the RAF airfield used in the Battle of Britain which was transferred to the US Air Force. The cast included Michael Redgrave, Trevor Howard, John Mills, Bonar Colleano and a very young Jean Simmons singing 'Let Him Go, Let Him Tarry'.

With the end of the war in sight by December 1944, many film producers were anxious to discard war themes and get back to making films for pure entertainment. With the Rank Organisation owning 619 cinemas in Britain and 442 other cinemas controlled by the Associated British Picture Corporation, a committee was set up to study the monopoly operating in the industry.

MGM-London, mindful of Alexander Korda's promise to create a Culver City in Britain, purchased the Amalgamated Studios at Elstree, near Borehamwood, from the Prudential Assurance Company. It was hoped that the studios, completed shortly before the war, would become the world's most up-to-date centre for film-making. In addition, 100 acres adjoining the site were bought for exterior shooting and necessary extensions. Korda promised to carry out his £35 million post-war production programme for MGM at the studios while making temporary use of the facilities at Denham where work was beginning on his new production, *Perfect Strangers*, initially directed by Wesley Ruggles and starring Deborah Kerr and Robert Donat.

While many prominent writers of the time – including Nevile Shute – were placed under contract to the studios, Korda's hopes of making Elstree the finest film complex in England never came to anything and he parted from MGM in 1946.

'During the filming of *Perfect Strangers*,' said Deborah Kerr, 'I moved to the English Speaking Union Club in London. It seemed a nice, safe, respectable place in which to live, but unfortunately they put me right at the top of the building. Every time I heard a flying bomb coming over I used to jump underneath the bed; I couldn't stand being underground, it made me claustrophobic.

'While I was at Denham making the picture, Lilli Palmer and her husband Rex Harrison were living in a house just across the road from the studios. They invited me in for a drink one evening and we were all sitting quietly in the front room when I heard what I thought sounded like a German aircraft. We listened to the noise of the engine, trying to determine whether it was a bomber or just a fighter, and there was no warning of any kind, just a terrifying explosion, and I said, "Christ! It's a bomb...and it sounded as if it landed right in the garden!" The doors were in splinters, every window was shattered and there was thick acrid dust everywhere. Rex was severely cut on the forehead. That will always be my most vivid memory of the war...I shook like a leaf when the all-clear went, ten minutes later, and I had nightmares about it for weeks afterwards. And for a very long time, any loud noise or the sudden sound of sirens terrified me and I hated that part of it.'

Meanwhile in 1944 in the Ardennes, a high rolling plateau with misty valleys and small villages, Sergeant Alan Badel – together with another sergeant of the Sixth Airborne Division – rescued a paratrooper right in the path of an advancing German 'Tiger' tank. Twenty-one-year-old Badel, not long married and straight out of drama school, volunteered to bring in the soldier who had been badly wounded by machine-gun fire from the tank. Throwing smoke grenades to give themselves cover, the sergeants dashed into the road, 100 yd from the tank and dragged the wounded paratrooper to safety.

Earlier that year Flying-Officer Donald Pleasance was forced to bale out of the Lancaster bomber in which he was wireless operator. Taken prisoner by the Germans, he spent the rest of the war in a prison camp in Western Pomerania, and when he came back to England he was hospitalised by the RAF, suffering from malnutrition. As soon as he was fit he went back to the theatre to take up a career that had started in 1939 in a summer season at the Playhouse Theatre, Jersey. Having played supporting roles in the West End, he went back in repertory, and after working at Birmingham and Perth he came back to London in 1951 to work regularly in films and on television, winning acclaim for his outstanding performance in Pinter's play, *The Caretaker*, in London and on Broadway.

Glenn Miller, staying at Bedford on account of the doodlebugs, flew towards Paris on 15 December 1944. He was going ahead of the band to make the hotel arrangements and they were to follow the next morning. The next day the band were told there was a cancellation because of bad weather and twenty-four hours later they were delayed yet another day.

Finally arriving at Orly airport outside Paris they waited for Miller but he never showed up. He had been missing a full thirty-six hours before anyone realised it.

For nearly three years his widow Helen refused to believe he was dead, and it wasn't until 1947 that she finally realised he wasn't going to come back.

The now-derelict runway at Tinwoods Farm, Bedfordshire, from which Miller's aircraft, the 'Norseman', took off, has become a place of pilgrimage for numbers of people of different nationalities who visit it each year. The service buildings and the control tower can still be seen.

Today Bedford farmer Alan Quenby, who leases the farmland from the Ministry of Defence, walks over the runway with Glenn Miller fans who talk to him about the music they remember, tunes like 'Moonlight Serenade' and 'Chatanooga Choo-Choo' and 'American Patrol'; and there's an occasional piece in a newspaper about a diver who thinks he has located the wreckage of the one-engined 'Norseman', or a fan who believes he has solved the mystery of the missing aircraft and of the disappearance of the gifted musician who enlisted in the American army to lead General Eisenhower's 'personal band'.

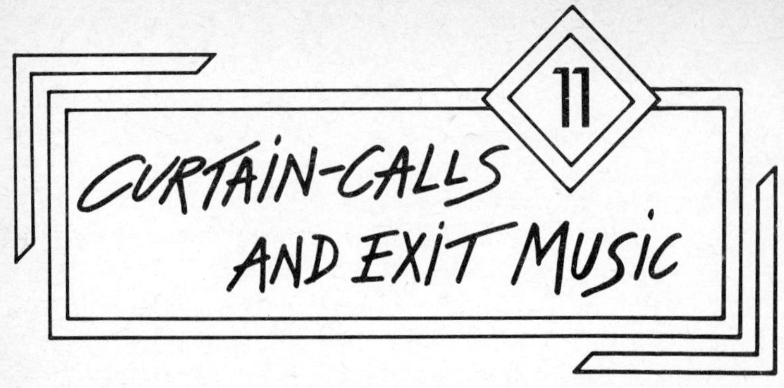

> In show business if you have a great opening and a great
> finish you don't have to apologise for all the dull stuff in
> the middle
>
> *George Burns (Comedian)*

The first demobbed soldiers walked out of their barracks in
their free demob suits in 1945, but the best-dressed men
were still those in uniform – although this presented problems of a kind, particularly for Lieutenant-Colonel Diggles
(Coldstream Guards) the newly appointed Deputy Provost
Marshal for Paris.

Down the elegant Rue Faubourg Saint Honoré walked
the strangest collection of uniforms the city had ever seen.
There was UNRRA (United Nations Relief and Rehabili-
tation Administration), ENSA, the FFI, in part GI battledress
and part Maquis field uniform; WAACs, WAAFs, WRNS
and assorted members of British and American armies;
and it was part of the Lieutenant-Colonel's job to decide
which of them merited a salute and which of them was
improperly dressed.

He soon gave up on ENSA, UNRRA, and the various
war correspondents, and tried to concentrate on the soldiers
of the British army. The first thing he saw from his office
window were two officers walking out of the main entrance
wearing correct dress in every detail, except for their

corduroy trousers. Indignant protests followed between Diggles and unit headquarters, but their Commanding Officer, Colonel Bill Marmion, soothingly poured the oil of compromise over the greying hairs of the Deputy Provost Marshal.

He explained that his men, of the Eleventh Hussars (the 'Cherry Pickers'), had fought in corduroy trousers from Alamein to the borders of the Third Reich. Surely they were entitled to a mere forty-eight hours of peace in Paris no matter how odd their pantaloons? It was agreed.

Diggles mopped his brow, put on his cap and left his office to join Parisians in the crowded street; they were cheering the RAF band of the Second Tactical Air Force, marching through the main streets to give an open-air concert in the Champs Elysées. After the concert they went back to a parachute training camp where an ENSA party entertained them. The troops, within forty-eight hours, were to make history. They were going to drop beyond the river Rhine in front of the Second Army.

The men enjoyed the show and joined in choruses of 'Silent Night', 'Roll Me Over', and 'Lilli Marlene' until it was time for them to 'chase the glowing hours with flying feet'.

In Hanover the civilian population was ordered to fight to the death as British troops entered the town, but the soldiers found them leaning placidly against notices proclaiming the need 'to defend the Fatherland to the last breath'. Tanks, trucks and large lorries moved in a steady procession with traffic jams extending for miles. Sandwiched between an armoured bulldozer and a massive tank were two small cars with banners on the sides, *Stars in Battledress* . . .

Back home, aircraftman Stanley Joseph, eldest son of Harry Joseph, the managing director of Leeds City Varieties Theatre, returned on seven days leave from Brussels. He had helped with the production of ENSA shows in Normandy.

Later, attached to the Allied First Airborne Army, he was far too busy for shows.

'The German services entertainments were very different from ours,' he said. 'Their shows always began with a political speech which was followed by a little heavy opera, and the finale was another political speech.'

Carroll Levis returned from his travels in North Africa and Europe saying that 'army talent could beat ENSA every-time as far as male entertainers were concerned but they couldn't supply glamour, which was wanted most of all. There seem to be hundreds of straight singers and crooners and pianists and Sergeant Bob Andrews (Royal Signals) was the Tommy Trinder of the Middle East, and due for stardom.

'Well,' said Andrews philosophically in the 1970s, 'it hasn't happened yet but I'm still hoping.'

Earlier in February the Duchess of Kent took her children to see *Goody Two Shoes* at the Coliseum and afterwards they all went backstage to meet the horse. Princess Alexandra asked if she could see the men inside the horse and her wish was duly granted.

Daphne Du Maurier's play *The Years Between* opened at Wyndham's Theatre; and twenty years after its original production, *Yellow Sands* was back in the West End at the Westminster, starring Sir Cedric Hardwicke. The theatre was under the management of Robert Donat, who defended the spate of revivals in a letter to the Press.

'I speak only for the revival of *Yellow Sands*, which I defend to the last barnacle and bit of seaweed, for the following reason: this comedy is of the earth at its earthiest and the sea at its saltiest. The barnacles and the seaweed are real because it's a sort of English folk play.'

The new play at the Savoy was *The Assassin*, by American writer Irwin Shaw, and it was about the murder on Christmas Eve 1942 of Admiral Darlan, High-Commissioner of North Africa and Commander-in-Chief of French Naval Forces. Barry Morse played the assassin and Henry Oscar was the French police chief; his first part after his years with

ENSA's Drama Division.

Laura Henderson's will was published. The owner of the Windmill Theatre had died on 29 November 1944, leaving £246,191. The majority of the shares went to her manager, Vivian Van Dam, but every employee working in the theatre at the time of her death received £10.

Tom O'Brien, then secretary of NATKE (National Association of Theatrical and Kinematographic Employees) announced that 'the theatrical profession was staggered by a report that Jack Hylton proposed to engage Maurice Chevalier to appear at the Victoria Palace for a salary of £1,000 a week.

'Hundreds of British artistes and scores of British stars were serving in the armed forces or working for ENSA at modest salaries and if the theatre had that kind of money to burn, then many of its underprivileged sections could do with it.'

Jack Hylton pointed out that Chevalier had been refused a visa to enter Britain: '... no reason was given and I am at a loss to understand it'. Earlier, Chevalier had been acquitted of a charge of collaborating with the Germans and had been booked by Hylton for a ten-week tour.

Ivor Novello's new musical, *Perchance to Dream*, went into rehearsal; it was to open at the London Hippodrome in April and run for 1,022 performances. Another long-running success was Esther McCracken's *No Medals* which had opened at the end of 1944 at the Vaudeville Theatre and went on until 1946, running for 742 performances, with Fay Compton, Valerie White and an actress from Morecambe making her debut in the West End, Thora Hird.

She remembers the play as 'her big break'. She had been living at Morecambe and working in repertory until *No Medals*.

'George Formby had seen me in a play at Morecambe and wanted me to do a film with him at Ealing Studios, but the producer felt the part needed an older woman and Beryl Mason got the part. But I did get a film contract out of it.

'We rang up early at the Vaudeville because the V-2s were still flying over. [The V-2 was the second of Hitler's V-weapons and the world's first rocket missile; 1,000 were dropped on London, more on Antwerp. The last fell in Kent in March 1945.]

'A V-2 dropped quite near the theatre one night, but none of the audience left so we just went on with the play. I also entertained the troops, doing a sort of off-the-cuff act with Bonar Colleano at the Nuffield Centre and the Stage Door Canteen. We were living in Ealing in those days and I hated it after Morecambe...I've never been sophisticated. Of course there were the doodlebugs and everything, and my husband was away most of the time in the RAF. When he was posted to Belgium I said as long as he comes back I won't grumble, even if he's wounded. Fortunately he came back all in one piece.

'When *No Medals* finished I was out of work for nearly twelve months; we sold our little house in Morecambe and brought Janette [Thora Hird's daughter] down to live in London. Then I was asked to do an audition at the New Lindsey Theatre – I'd never done one before – and got a part in *Flowers for the Living*. It was a Cinderella story after that, offers from all over the place and I've been acting now for well over thirty years.

'I never went to acting school, I was born into one because my father used to work at the old Royalty Theatre in Morecambe. He always told me to rehearse properly: "Never insult the public by being unrehearsed." There's so many things to learn in this business and I enjoy learning them and I'm blessed with a husband who really does manage me. As he says, I've been called a real professional many times but never a pretty face. Mind you I think there are lots of character women around who just aren't seen in the right part at the right time.

'We have a little cottage in the country now and stay there at weekends. Janette [Scott] is blissfully happy, married to a real professional – Mel Tormé, the singer – and they live in Cold Water Canyon, Beverly Hills, with our little grand-daughter. Jan doesn't act any more; she once said that if she had married a greengrocer, and she would have if she loved him, she'd probably have gone on with her career.'

Janette Scott was formerly married to Canadian singer Jackie Rae in the 1960s; her name was also linked with David Frost in 1962 when he was beginning his meteoric rise to television stardom; in 1945 he was an alert little four-year-old, attending a kindergarten school in Bedford, 'showing promise of good ability'.

Gladys Cooper was back in London from Hollywood in March 1945 and appeared in a special broadcast, *Fanfare*, from the Stage Door Canteen; and Josephine Baker made her first appearance in London for eight years in front of an audience of 1,500 factory workers. It was her first time before civilian war workers and she sang songs that had made her famous and led the audience in community singing.

The Old Vic company prepared to tour liberated Europe with Dame Sybil Thorndike, Margaret Leighton, Joyce Redman, Laurence Olivier and Ralph Richardson; Henry Hall and his band, Heather Thatcher, and Basil Radford were already in France. Cicely Courtneidge was in Gibraltar, entertaining the troops with Thorley Walters and Hartley Power.

On the overseas scene, Roosevelt died on 12 April and Harry Truman, the 'unimpressive little man' from Kansas City, was appointed President; he was to make one of the most momentous decisions in history and alter forever the course of civilisation. In the same April, Lieutenant-Commander Gerald Ford was serving on an aircraft carrier; Lieutenant-Commander Richard Nixon had just returned to America from the South Pacific and another sailor, John Fitzgerald Kennedy, was in a Florida hospital for wounded officers.

In Hollywood, Shirley Temple married for the first time, and Lauren Bacall agreed to become Mrs Humphrey Bogart.

Mary Honri recalled the night she was with an ENSA show, entertaining 250 British troops guarding Belsen together with the same number of French soldiers released from that terrible place.

'Somehow,' she said, 'I managed to give a bilingual show. After I'd finished singing "God Save the King" and the "Marseillaise" the French all crowded round me and said I was the first woman in evening dress they had seen in five years ... tears were streaming down their cheeks and even the British colonel in charge blew his nose very hard.'

She went over the camp and what she saw she never forgot: it measured 1 mile by 600 yd with possibly just enough room for 8,000 people. Although 40,000 people were still alive in 1945, 10,000 bodies, unburied and twisted by death into grotesque positions, lay rotting in the sunshine. Of the 40,000, 200 of them were children and there were also 25,000 women, Jewesses and partisans from all over Europe. The men were either Jewish or else political prisoners, some of them convicted of the crime of listening to BBC broadcasts on the radio.

Death came from systematic starvation and typhus, of which there were 800 cases. During April 13,000 people died of various illnesses, and six weeks later there were still more than 11,000 in hospital. Of 60 huts in the camp, 15 were used by 70 SS guards, and 600 to 1,000 prisoners were crowded in a hut meant to hold 60. The sole water supply was a stagnant pond and prisoners were forced to drag the dead to communal graves in the compound; they were so weak it took four of them to carry one corpse. Although 2,000 men worked twelve hours a day to clear away the dead, 10,000 still lay unburied, dead from starvation, shooting, some beaten to death, while others were the victims of diseases like typhus.

Rations consisted of one cup of synthetic ('ersatz') coffee in the morning, and a noon meal of a little turnip soup, sometimes supplemented by a few ounces of bread. Many had received no food at all until the British troops arrived;

the place was finally destroyed by flamethrowers some months later.

Anna Neagle, who toured Europe with Rex Harrison in *French Without Tears* for ENSA in 1945, says that two things stand out vividly in her mind from that time: a visit made to the Edith Cavell Institute in Brussels, where some of the victims of the concentration camps were being nursed back to life; and at Eindhoven in Holland, being taken to the Red Cross train bringing back hundreds of displaced persons and former prisoners of the Nazis. She remembered what she had seen when she played Odette GC after the war.

Dame Sybil Thorndike, who had been bombed out of her Chelsea flat in 1944, was in Paris with the Old Vic during the summer: 'We played in the Comédie Française; it was the first time an English company had played there and what a glorious theatre it was. Lewis [Casson] was also there, directing a production of *St Joan* at the Marigny Theatre, with our daughter Ann Casson.

'Joyce Redman and Margaret Leighton were with me and we all spent a weekend with the Fifth Scottish Division, the colonel was a cousin of mine. We had a wonderful time in a lovely French château there.

'We all had to wear that ENSA uniform in the heat of Paris, and it was dreadful walking about the streets in the sun. So in the end they gave us permission to take off our jackets; we could go out in the blouses as long as the sleeves were carefully rolled up.

'When we finished the play, I stayed on to do some recitals with Robert Speight and finally came back to the Old Vic. I remember meeting so many interesting people in Paris but it was a long time ago. It's a strange thing that although I'm over ninety now, I can always remember lines but not people's names.

'Looking back on the war we had such wonderful times and did the type of work I enjoy so much. I enjoyed it because in a way it was like working in a fit-up company and one felt very close to the audience, and one was able to have such rapport with them. Although none of us got much more than a soldier's pay, it didn't matter – and they entertained us so well in those miners' homes.'

John Fernald produced *Gaslight* for ENSA with Deborah Kerr and Stewart Granger. 'It was most exciting,' said Deborah Kerr, 'as I had never been out of England before. I had lunch not too long ago with Nan Culver, who played the maid in *Gaslight*, and she said: "How did we ever exist through all that?"

'It was quite an experience. First the boat across to France and then by road to Brussels where we were due to open. No one ever seemed to know we were arriving and so it was pretty chaotic.

'We played Eindhoven – I had a letter just the other day from a man who'd been in the paratroops in Holland and he mentioned he'd seen *Gaslight* there. I think I saw more of the war in Holland than anywhere else: crosses by the side of the road, wrecked cars and tanks, pale-faced children pressed against shop windows or staring at us from the doors of damaged houses. They had suffered a great deal there.

'In Paris we played in the Theatre Champs Elysées, and they allowed us to use the Officers Club in Faubourg St Honoré. That's where I ran into the Sadler's Wells Ballet and it was marvellous to see Margot Fonteyn and all the others. It was "Hello, Hello!" all round and I told Ninette de Valois that I'd been one of her students at the beginning of the war.

'"And you're now an actress," she said, "how very wise of you to change your mind."

'I think we returned to London via Brussels. I do know we played there twice and all the troops enjoyed the play immensely, especially being able to hiss at Stewart Granger as the villain. We met all the top brass at Monty's headquarters.

'To me the whole thing was something different, and while it might have meant the temporary suspension of a career, it was such a worthwhile job.'

Four days after Germany surrendered, Pat Kirkwood and her mother flew by Clipper to Baltimore, en route to Hollywood: 'We went by train from Baltimore and it had beds and baths and every luxury although mother didn't think much of the staff. She asked for sauce and they brought her salt.

'It was hard to find somewhere to stay in Hollywood, but I left it to mother and she found a strange little house not far from the MGM studios in Culver City. I'm sure the executives there thought we were a couple of eccentrics with our shabby suitcases, old fur coats and two new hats we had bought in Baltimore.

'I was due to make a picture with Van Johnson or Robert Walker and I was cast as an American crooner, with Van Johnson – as it turned out – as a marine. As soon as I read the script of *No Leave, No Love* I knew it was awful, and then I heard the director appointed by the studio had never made a film before so I went to my agent Johnny Hyde [later Marilyn Monroe's agent] in desperation and told him I couldn't do it.

' "You have to do it," he said. "If you don't, they'll suspend you."

' "What does that mean?" I asked him.

' "That means you get no pay, baby."

'I did the film. Kay Thompson gave me lessons on how to talk "American" and they wanted to dye my hair blonde and alter my teeth but I wouldn't allow it. Van Johnson was very kind to me. He said, "This movie has all the makings of a first-class stinker so let's just sit back and enjoy it."

'Eventually we finished making it and he was right, it was bad. I came home in 1947 and went straight into *Starlight Roof* at the Hippodrome with Vic Oliver, Fred Emney and little Julie Andrews, and it ran for two years. It was wonderful being back in London then with the war over at last, although I had to wait until 1949 to see my name in lights . . . in Noel Coward's *Ace of Clubs*.'

Moscow celebrated the victory in Europe with a dazzling

display of fireworks and every searchlight in the city was switched on; the sky flared into a blaze of lights as hundreds of yellow, mauve and purple rockets shot high above the rooftops. The main feature of the display was a huge portrait of Stalin suspended from a balloon with floodlights focussed on it from every corner of Moscow.

Meanwhile, what was happening on the Asian front? Frank Tinsdale served with the RAF in Bengal, Burma and the Cocos Islands, but saw no ENSA shows until 1944, by which time the Burma campaign was set on the road to victory.

'There was a great deal of criticism about it but I thought the lack of professional entertainment was due to the fact that other areas had higher priorities than we did.

'I've always regretted that Vera Lynn was taken ill in Calcutta when she was due to visit us as I was one of the aircrew detailed to fly her in. Our first concert from ENSA starred "Stainless" Stephen who endeared himself to the chaps by going round all the aircraft as they were being prepared for operations, chatting to the crews as they worked. He even helped them push 1,000lb bombs around, a heavy job for an elderly gentleman in the humid heat of Bengal.

'During his show in the camp cinema – a bamboo and thatch hut – the generator broke down, so a sergeant climbed a support pole and jammed himself against a roof strut with an aircraft Aldiss lamp in his right hand, lighting the stage for the rest of the evening. He walked around bent double for ten days afterwards.'

For over a year a small party of girls risked the dangers and diseases of the Burma front to take entertainment to jungle troops in advanced units. They were the 'Besa Belles', part of the Bengal Entertainment for Services Association, with seventeen companies touring British and Indian camps and RAF units in Bengal, Assam and Burma. One company on its way to give a concert to troops in a recently occupied

Burmese village nearly fell into Japanese hands when their bus took a wrong turning.

A Sergeant Peter Felsham who acted as compère at a forward base said: 'We called them the "Jungle Follies". To us they were the five prettiest girls that ever came out of Calcutta, and when we knew they were going to give us a show we rigged up the stage just like the old Chiswick Empire, with all kinds of coloured spots and genuine footlights. The girls had to travel 200 miles from the nearest railway and they managed to bring all their own props and costumes with them on a truck; they even had a piano and as far as we were concerned, they were a colossal success.'

Warrant Officer Bill Sutton had gone to India to organise some RAF *Gang Shows* for the Burma front. His sergeant was a musician who had worked with Eric Winstone and Harry Gold before joining the RAF; his name was Norrie Paramor, now the musical director of the BBC Midland Orchestra. Another member of an early *Gang Show* in India was Airman Peter Sellers.

Born in Southsea, he had been evacuated to Ilfracombe when the war broke out and his first job was as a drummer with Waldini's band. Said Bill Sutton: 'Peter worked with us as a mimic, but he was just beginning and very raw in those days.

'After the show we were invariably dragged off to the officers' or sergeants' mess for a drink. One night there was a party in some officers' mess and Peter – who played a group captain in one of the sketches – appeared in the middle of the party in the bloody uniform, complete with "Flying Officer Kite" type moustache. He was quite good until he got drunk and gave the game away. The commanding officer took umbrage and the whole *Gang Show* unit was put on a fizzer. That took some sorting out, but fortunately there was an understanding air commodore in welfare and he realised that entertainers found it difficult to conform to air-force discipline. I must say he was always a great help when we were in trouble; a diplomatic telephone call or two, the unit was moved on somewhere else, and all was forgiven and forgotten. And, thank God, we never stayed too long anywhere.

'The ethics of command as far as the *Gang Shows* were concerned were that all offences were dealt with at head-quarters. There seemed to be a greater sense of responsibility among our chaps and I think they all felt they were doing something useful. Ralph [Reader] was the guv'nor and everyone called him by his first name. Even when I reached the dizzy heights of warrant officer rank I was still Bill to the boys.

'We were all paid RAF pay but they allowed us to do a maximum of four outside shows we could organise for ourselves to get money for make-up, laundry, stage clothes and the odd meal.

'It was agreed by the Air Ministry that we could appear in a commercial theatre as a *RAF Gang Show*. We were in many ways a spearhead in service entertainment, and even played to US troops who seemed to appreciate the British sense of humour.

'Looking back it was an experience you could never forget; it rubbed the sharp corners off. Certainly there were moments of black despair when all you wanted to do was get as far away from the shows as possible, and so we changed the units round quite a bit, putting in experienced men and transferring key men to new units. Each unit had an individual programme with Ralph writing most of the material.

'Naturally they gradually broke up when the European war ended, and by the time 1946 was over all the units were disbanded.

'A typical show would open with a number of cross-talk gags and then we'd go into some sketches and finish the first half with a musical finale. Because we were playing to servicemen we worked in a lot of air-force patter and topical comment. The humour was broad, sometimes a little coarse, but there were also serious items in the second half from fine singers and musicians and the sentimental ballads always went over big.

'My unit used to finish the first act with a medley of popular songs, with Bill Dickie, the singer, coming on in drag for a Florrie Ford number. In the front row sat all the officers, local notables and the padre and all their respective wives; and one night Bill sang his song and followed it with a little "knees-up" dance down to the footlights.

'Backstage we could hear hysterical screams coming from the audience and we'd no idea what was going on: Bill had completely forgotten to put his jock-strap and underpants on. He realised something was wrong and rushed off into the wings to the loudest applause of the evening, led – I was told later by the adjutant – by the padre's wife.

'Tony Hancock was with us, another rank raw amateur with hopeless nerves, but we kept him on because he was such a nice fellow; Graham Stark was another amateur, he was in the same unit as Hancock in 1945. Then there was Joe Black, the comic; Reg Dixon; Harry Dawson, the singer; Charles Gray, the actor; Albert Locke who's now with television as an executive; Len Lowe; Tony Melody; Stan Mortensen, the ex-footballer; Rex Jameson, who does a drag act as "Mrs Shufflewick"; Dick Emery, of course, and Jill Knight who is the Member of Parliament for Edgbaston in Birmingham.'

A close friend of Tony Hancock, writer Philip Oakes is quite certain that had Hancock lived 'and stayed off the booze, he would have been not only a comic of world stature but a very fine actor too.

'We were very close friends, although – as you may imagine – we had our quarrels. I'm quite sure he had the greatest talent as a performer I've ever encountered and the comedy he created was both instant and lasting. I miss him still.'

Eddie Joffe, the television director was working in the television studios with Tony Hancock in Sydney in 1968, by which time he had become a renowned comedian, when the executives wanted to cancel the show because of Hancock's excessive drinking.

'Tony was put in hospital,' said Eddie, 'and they wanted me to tell him: "One more drink and you're on the first plane back to the UK." The doctor suggested he should stay with us when he came out of hospital; we had two separate flats and his part wasn't furnished so we put some stuff in it for him.

'That night, 24 June 1968, we went out to dinner, leaving him in the upstairs apartment – he was invited but didn't want to come. When we got back, I was very tired and couldn't remember whether his lights were on or not.

'The next morning we banged on the ceiling to wake him up but there was no reply. The kids used to call him "Mr Helicopter" so I said to the eldest: "Go and wake Mr Helicopter up for me." Then my wife went upstairs but it was too late. He died from a combination of pills and drink.'

Jill Knight first became involved with the *Gang Show* when she was with the WAAFs in Germany. A *Gang Show* unit came over and they were one girl short, so she joined them. She had already done some singing and dancing at service concerts 'just for fun' and had also written a few songs herself. She toured with the *Gang Show* and did some broadcasting on the British Forces Network radio in Hamburg. 'I did think of doing it professionally after the war; I'd gone straight into the WAAFs from school, but instead I married an ex-naval chap and joined the Young Conservatives.' She became a Member of Parliament in 1966 and was awarded the MBE in 1969 for public services in Northampton – where she still lives.

Jack Hawkins, who died in July 1973, was second-in-command of Bren-gun carriers in the 1st battalion of his regiment, the Royal Welch Fusiliers, when he first went to India in 1942; but he was soon organising concert parties for the division. When ENSA arrived, he was the obvious choice for organiser, and eventually became Colonel-in-

Charge of ENSA administration for India and SEAC.

'I was based mainly in Bombay at the beginning,' he recalled in 1972, 'and later on we went to Calcutta, but my territory stretched from Karachi to Hong Kong.'

He first met his wife, Doreen, in India when she was touring in one of the earliest ENSA companies to entertain the 'Forgotten Army'. The billet where Doreen and another actress (now the Hon Mrs Gerald Lascelles) were accommodated in Rangoon had previously been a Japanese brothel, but Jack Hawkins 'managed to make it fairly comfortable. One had to do the best one could in those days.'

The only trouble he experienced was with ENSA parties fresh out from the UK or companies from the Middle East: 'Quite often they seemed to send us the difficult people from Egypt, and of course as soon as the European war was over they all wanted to come out.

'It was difficult to explain the situation properly; it wasn't possible to go to the army unless they could walk 500 miles and even if they made it, they'd just be a bloody nuisance. They couldn't entertain up there.

'There was the typical ENSA comedian who would say to me: "Now, look here, old chap. I must go up to the front line right away. I've got no time to spare because George Black – or Jack Hylton or Firth Shephard – wants me and I have to be back in London in three weeks time."

'I'd maintain a tactful silence for a moment and then he'd say: "You don't believe me, do you?" And wearily I'd say, "No, I don't believe you."'

It was Sir Richard Attenborough who said in tribute to him that 'Jack Hawkins was not only one of the finest actors on the British screen but also one of the most courageous men I have ever met or am ever likely to meet. We who loved and admired him will miss him greatly; his wit, his gentleness, his courage and his humour.'

Patrick Cargill was out in India in 1942, posted to a reserve regiment when the Burma Road was at its peak. 'All the people I went out with were sent forward while

I sat in the depot in a sort of limbo, doing neither one thing nor the other. Then the commanding officer, who had gone through the ranks and used to boast that he could spot a footballer or an actor, appointed me entertainments officer. He told everyone not to worry about my long hair as I was an actor, but they must all obey me nevertheless.

'I set up an inter-regimental radio link and did a production of *The Importance of Being Earnest*. A stage production followed and naturally theatre, stage, lights, costumes were all made from nothing. Lots of chaps considered us plain exhibitionists on the unit, but lots more were keen to join us. The only reason I chose that particular play was I'd seen the London production with Edith Evans, Peggy Ashcroft, John Gielgud and Jack Hawkins. It was terribly difficult to get a script from Delhi and then to cut it reasonably well both for the broadcast and the live performance.

'There were privates, corporals, sergeants and warrant officers all participating in the entertainment set-up, and I was able to bring together these enthusiastic amateurs and put on a good show in a very static regiment where soldiers passed through regularly on their way to almost certain death in Burma. Those who came back had suffered a great deal and they weren't easy to entertain.

'It was a desolate place called Ranchi, absolutely at the other end of the world. When the war finally came to an end, people went away, we were disbanded and everyone wanted to go home. I was discharged from the army in 1946 and afterwards I did repertory in different parts of the country and toured *Mountain Air* for CEMA in 1949 in Germany for the BAOR (British Army of Occupation on the Rhine). Then came the West End with *High Spirits* at the London Hippodrome in 1953.'

Donald Sinden toured throughout SEAC with ENSA in *Normandy Story* (originally called *French Leave*). With him in the company were Winifred Shotter and Lawrence O'Madden. When O'Madden had to fly back to England to make the film *Lisbon Story*, Major Michael Brennan,

Officer-in-Charge of ENSA in Burma took over his part.

'We toured from Calcutta,' said Donald Sinden, 'and eventually reached Burma. I remember I got back to India a little late; I knew we had to leave Calcutta on the 9.30 train for Bombay and unfortunately I got to the station at 9.35 and the train had pulled out. It was a three-day journey and there was no train after that until next morning.

'When I finally hot-footed it into Bombay, an ENSA official met me to say the company had boarded the boat without me and I'd just have to wait for the next sailing in four weeks time. Within hours, or so it seemed, John Gielgud had arrived with an ENSA company to present *Hamlet* and he was short of an actor to play the Ghost. I thought this would be a wonderful opportunity for me; I was available and he was quite willing for me to join the company. But the same ENSA chap who had met me said: "No, sorry. Sinden's passage home has already been booked and he has to go." So I wasn't able to join the Gielgud tour.'

On 6 August 1945 the atomic bomb was dropped on Hiroshima, and three million leaflets floated down to tell the Japanese that the Americans 'were in possession of the most destructive weapon ever designed by man. A single one of our atomic bombs equals the explosive power carried by 2,000 Super-Fortresses. This is an awful fact for you to ponder. We have just begun to use this weapon.

'Before using this bomb again and again to destroy every resource which your military leaders have, to prolong this useless war, we ask you now to petition your emperor to end the war. Take steps now or we shall resolutely employ this bomb promptly and forcefully.'

With the dropping of the bomb in the closing stages of the war, events moved a lot quicker than people had anticipated; and on 14 August Japan surrendered unconditionally to the Allies. As far as many entertainers were concerned it was time to say goodbye to services entertainment, although the *Nagpur Times* of 18 August stated that: 'The announcement of Japan's acceptance of the Allied peace terms does not mean that ENSA will immediately down props and go home. Rather will it tend to step up its programme and work with renewed vigour to see that while men of the services remain here they will still have entertainment.'

In fact it wasn't until October that ENSA arrived in Singapore and then it was in the formidable shape of Mrs Barbara Ireland-Smith, Senior Welfare Supervisor who had first arrived there on 5 September, three hours after the formal surrender on board HMS Sussex, when she began looking for suitable premises for the organisation: 'I made a tour of prison camps and also made inquiries about sending in small parties to entertain in the camps. The commandants at Changi, Sian and Krangi were anxious for us to lay on something as soon as possible as many of the prisoners were ill and awaiting transport and any relaxation was welcome.

'In Krangi, conditions were beyond description and although they managed to form their own orchestra and set up their own theatre the Japanese had refused them permission to stage any entertainment.'

With Major Macdonald of RAPWI Control she decided to raid a Jap store in the jungle because 'forty men were dying from malnutrition and we had heard that there was tons of dried milk in that particular dump'. At times it was necessary to produce a Bren gun to secure entry past the Japanese, but it was in this manner that Mrs Ireland-Smith secured her first transport, a dilapidated old Morris Ten: 'The stores of milk and so forth were acquired using the same method and we rushed all we could to Krangi and Sian Road camp where many children were in captivity.'

The inspection of the Victoria Theatre followed as a matter of course and after careful cleaning it was soon made ready for its first ENSA show, *Keep Moving*.

And theatre critic Abdul Rahman Siddiqui, writing from his local paper located at 24 Chowringhee, told the people that when ENSA's *Strike Up the Band* came to India, he did not intend to miss it. 'This team, a merry company of eleven, has a blonde, Irish Jewel by name, a crooner and one amusing item of hers is a song entitled "Too Old for Toys and Too Young for Boys". Enticing is it not? The company also has Virginia Rose a dancer who has danced for ENSA in many lands. The accompanying band will include in their repertoire a particularly appealing arrangement of "The Holy City." '

Eight young ENSA girls were the first white women to land on the Cocos Islands for 120 years; members of Waldini's band, they entertained servicemen based on the islands for a week before going on to Rangoon. Gracie Fields also visited the islands, after playing Singapore and Manila. In Bombay she announced she intended to retire at the end of her tour saying: 'You can tell Rochdale I'm too old to swing my legs around. After a three week break on Capri I'll go back to France and Germany and then home to see the folks and sing to them. Then I'll go back to my villa and start playing house.'

Frank Tinsdale, who was on the Cocos Islands at the time, didn't agree that Gracie was too old to swing her legs around.

'It was when we were flying supply missions to Malaya, Singapore and what was then French and Dutch Indonesia, that Gracie Fields came to entertain us with Monty Banks. She gave us a wonderful show on our open-air stage, turning some magnificent cartwheels to show she hadn't lost the knack.

'I had the pleasure of helping her into a parachute-harness before she left the Cocos in a Liberator bomber. I was told later by the flight-engineer on her aircraft that they lost power in one engine as they became airborne, and there were moments of terrible tension until it picked up again. Liberators normally sank immediately on impact with the sea and that part of the Indian Ocean was heavily infested with sharks. There would have been no hope for anyone on board if the aircraft had gone into the water ... I have often wondered if Gracie was ever told of her narrow escape.'

When Gracie Fields was in Borneo, singing to a large group of soldiers at a place called Tarrakan, there seemed to her to be thousands of uniformed men sitting on the ground and along the slope of a steep hill, and she was told some of them had stayed up all night not to miss the show. She asked the boys all to light a match or a cigarette lighter and to turn around quickly and see a scene they'd remember all their lives. They did as she asked and saw the thousands of lights going way up to the top of the mountain, and as Gracie said: 'It really was something.'

They told her later that some Japs had been watching the whole thing. She was given a souvenir of her visit, a heart-shaped brooch, inscribed: 'To our Gracie, from the boys on Tarrakan, 1945'. Made from part of a Japanese aircraft, she keeps it with her wherever she goes, together with another precious souvenir, a silver serviette ring from the boys on Balakpan, in Borneo.

In Bougainville she was taken to a clearing in the jungle where 25,000 troops were gathered and a general addressed them: 'Men, the Japanese have surrendered and I'm now going to ask Miss Gracie Fields if she will sing for all of us "The Lord's Prayer".'

As she began the song, men started taking their caps off and stood silently, under the hot sun, heads bowed as each note carried across the silence of the jungle and over the lowered heads. 'They seemed almost to have held their breath as I sang,' said Gracie. 'It was the most privileged and cherished moment of my life. And for years afterwards I received letters from some of the boys who remembered me singing "The Lord's Prayer" in Bougainville.'

She went back to Capri from a farewell performance at Maraad Barracks, in Kubri, near Cairo. The concert was compèred by Brian Reece and she told the correspondent of the *Egyptian Mail*: 'I don't think they realise at home just how much the lads here in the Middle East still need entertainments. Far too many of us have got the idea that after El Alamein, everybody left. I would have liked to have sung to fifty times as many boys as were here tonight.'

She was asked her opinion on ENSA and said that 'there has been far too much said against ENSA. During the whole time I've been with them, I've had a perfect time and we've played to the finest audiences in the world, the troops.'

Faith Brook arrived back in London, was given two weeks leave, and told she was being sent to India.

'Perhaps it was the tedious business of all those inoculations and vaccines; possibly the prospect of playing *Someone at the Door* again for what would be like an eternity, or maybe it was merely strain and exhaustion; anyway it led to my cracking up. I was by no means the only one and I had lasted out longer than some, but finally crack up I did.

'The army must have thought I was malingering and I was interviewed by at least six psychiatrists before they agreed to let me have treatment. This consisted of a fortnight's sleep with breathing exercises. Then I went up before a board of she-dragons dressed as ATS officers to be invalided out.

' "And what do you intend to do in civilian life?" asked the most formidable dragon. I said I hoped to continue as an actress, perhaps join a good repertory company.

' "How will you get a job as an actress?"

'I told them I knew a lot of people in the profession; that I'd been born into it and had made a good many contacts.

' "Who, for example?"

' "My father, for example," I said.

' "And who, pray, is your father?"

' "Clive Brook."

'In a flash the atmosphere altered, the icy air thawed and I was amongst the girls. They began to twitter and simper together. It was edging on the grotesque; the dragons had changed into house sparrows. No more difficulties, no more questions; VIP treatment, and I was finally out of battledress. I hurried out of the building; if I was going to be sick, I'd be sick in the open air.'

On 2 September, The Reverend Sir Herbert Dunnico, ENSA's Vice-President, resigned from the chairmanship of the public relations council and Naafi's broadcasting council. In office since 1940 he said: 'It has been a one-man dictatorship with absolute power and no one could appeal against the decisions.'

Basil Dean, still busy with shows in both the Middle and Far East, said he would reply later.

Labour member of Parliament for Doncaster, Evelyn Walkden, decided to join Dunnico – and Archie de Bear, who had also smartly jumped off the bandwagon. He did public relations until he decided that 'the Treasury and Naafi would have to sort out the shambles at Drury Lane, which in my view was cluttered by mismanagement and make-believe'. Basil Dean's secretary, Elizabeth Avaun, looked around her, sniffed the wind, and handed in her notice.

In October, in the House of Commons, the endearing Mr Walkden asked if Mr Morrison (later Lord Morrison of Lambeth), the Lord President of the Council, did not think it time ENSA was demobilised rather than that time, energy and money should be wasted on further activities. Mr Morrison, who had previously replied to another searching question concerning the activities of ENSA, replied: 'That is another question.'

Two days later he was asked by Sir Waldron Smithers (Conservative) if he would set up an inquiry under the chairmanship of a British judge at which evidence could be taken under oath to inquire into and report to the House the reasons for the criticisms and complaints on the working of ENSA. Morrison replied: 'No, sir.'

Said Smithers: 'Don't you realise that the question of scandal connected with ENSA is bigger than ENSA itself?'

Replied Morrison: 'I think you are making very heavy weather of it. The type of inquiry you suggest is a very heavy-handed affair.'

In a written answer to the inquisitive Sir Waldron, the War Minister, Mr Lawson, said that the total cost of ENSA entertainments at home and abroad, excluding India and Burma, in the six years that ended 6 August 1945 was £14,877,000. Of this, about £2,167,000 was borne by the Exchequer for entertainment in munition factories and – to a small extent – for the American forces under a reciprocal-aid agreement. Of the remaining £12,710,000, about £7,889,000 – the amount for the first five years – had been charged against Naafi surplus revenue.

In November, Herbert Morrison – replying in the House of Commons to E. P. Smith (Conservative Member for Ashford), said that the National Service Board was of the opinion that there was no need for a public inquiry into ENSA's activities. The services authorities considered that the scope of ENSA's activities and the enormous difficulties they had to face in bringing entertainment to forces all over the world had been insufficiently appreciated. It was only natural that there should have been local criticism, but viewed as a whole, the work of the organisation has been highly commendable.

Basil Dean said that ENSA would officially end on 30 June 1946; the adjutant-general announced that it had been decided to finish ENSA on 31 August 1946.

The last performance by a star under the auspices of ENSA took place in India when Tommy Trinder played a garrison theatre there ... and a young dancer, back from a nine-month tour of the Middle East, was able to give a performer's point of view:

'What ever they may say about Basil Dean, ENSA looked after the song-and-dance people very well. In Greece and Malta, we stayed at the best hotels, with private baths, excellent meals, breakfast in bed and a private beach for bathing. There were even iced drinks during the show ... Although we were supposed to be back in bed by midnight, the hostel matron was understanding and the rules were few and sensible. For one thing we weren't allowed to travel from a camp back to the hostel in anything other than the official bus. Well, girls are offered all kinds of lifts and they didn't want anyone to be stranded . . .or worse.

'I thought the pay was very good: I received £8 a week, but prices in the Middle East were ridiculous; £5 for a lipstick and £20 for a bathing cap. We were able to save a little because meals and accommodation were free, but I do think they should have done something about the medical services. Skin diseases were very common and the medical officers were very careless. They forgot greasepaint has to go on every night, aggravating the least skin eruption. A friend of mine developed impetigo and after pestering an army doctor for weeks, eventually got some ointment but it only made it worse. She was eventually cured by an American doctor, but unfortunately scars were left because of the delay and that can be a disaster for anyone in this business.

'It was terribly hard work. Dancing is the last thing you wanted to do in an airless oven heat, the air thick with large peculiar flies. One or two people in our company – I think they only joined ENSA to see new places and meet some officers – quarrelled with the authorities and were sent back home straight away. But I've found, since joining ENSA, I've been happier than I ever believed it possible to be.

'Think of it . . . simply for doing the job I was trained for in front of huge, appreciative audiences, I've seen Algiers, Greece, Italy, Sardinia . . . places I'd never have got to otherwise. I wasn't in Rome long enough to see St Peter's or in Athens long enough to do the ruins, but I've travelled for hours dressed in a sunsuit sitting on top of a lorry going along some of the loveliest roads in the world. I've eaten with arabs in bazaars, had marvellous parties and eaten strange food.

'Take it from me, all this grousing about ENSA doesn't come from us rank-and-file buskers and we were the ones who did the really hard work.

'I'm off to Burma and Japan next week and I don't care if ENSA goes on forever.'

'I wouldn't have missed any of it,' says international funny man Freddie Sales. 'It was wonderful. I saw places I never thought I'd see in a million years and met people I'll remember for the rest of my life. Little things I remember: the meal in the open-air in Italy with former prisoners-of-war playing guitars and accordions and singing songs about love and freedom and the sun; the businessman in Vienna who offered me £10 for a bottle of lime juice for his sick children and couldn't understand when I wouldn't accept the money; the chef at the hostel in Naples who served his apprenticeship in Brighton and would sit and talk about England as though it was his home.

'Flying from Sardinia to Corsica to put on an extra show at a remote camp and finding it had seven men and one officer and every villager in Ajaccio invited, filling the Nissen hut to capacity; the German boy in Krumpendorf who spat at me every day and said "Englander". And the day I spat back and said: "*Schweinhund!*" He wouldn't leave us alone after that and he cried when we said goodbye ...

'Arriving to do a show at a military hospital after a miserable week in a terrible hostel with awful food; driving for miles in an old truck with cold winds cutting through the canvas flaps ...

'Getting ready for the show, groaning, grumbling and longing to get back to London ... and then going on for the opening number ...

'The front row, a solid line of wheel-chairs and the men sitting in them were all amputees; every one of them had lost both legs and some were left with just an arm; but the look on their faces positively glowing with pleasurable anticipation ... Well, we worked as we had never worked before and there wasn't a grumble from any of us for the rest of the tour.

'And if my boy ever says, "What did you do during the war, dad?" I'll hunt out my ENSA badge and tell him all about it.'

Freddie is now starring in the *Spectacular Bicentennial Show* at The Dunes, Las Vegas (on a three-year contract), and after a recent appearance on the *Merv Griffin Show* on American television his career seems set for a lasting success.

There was a wartime film, adapted from the poem by Alice Duer Miller, called *The White Cliffs of Dover* (in which Elizabeth Taylor had a small part). At a high point in the picture, Irene Dunne, as the American girl who comes to love England, says: 'A life is a very, very long time when you look back to when you were young ...'

'When we were young,' says Constance Cummings, 'there was that comforting cliché, "as safe as houses", but it became rather a sour joke during the war. A landmine came down near here once and blew all the windows in. Someone telephoned to ask if I was all right and I said, "Yes, except for my windows", and we went into gales of laughter. As long as nobody was hurt, you didn't ask any more. I must say I'm glad I didn't miss it although I wouldn't wish it on anyone again. I just wish we could somehow recapture the *spirit* people had then.'

A tablet in bronze was unveiled to that 'spirit' on 8 November 1945 on the exterior wall of the London Hippodrome. Presented by the Variety Clubs of America, it read:

> To the everlasting honour of those British and
> American performers who, during the darkest days of
> the London blitz – when steadfastness and sheer courage
> counted as weapons of war – remembered the slogan
> of their profession ... 'Tonight and every night, the
> show must go on.'

When the Hippodrome was transformed into the 'Talk of the Town' restaurant some years ago, the tablet vanished from sight and has never been seen since.